Is Kate

She swallo

burned his rose today," she rasped, wondering why she felt the need to tell McCall.

"Oh?"

"It was the–the last rose he gave me. I–I had kept it in my Bible."

"Are you saying it's time for me to burn some roses?"

"Not necessarily. I just thought. . ."

DEBRA WHITE SMITH lives in east Texas with her husband and two small children. She is a writer, editor, and speaker who pens books and magazine articles, and has twenty-three book sales to her credit, both fiction and nonfiction. Debra holds a B.A. and M.A. in English. Both she and her novels have been voted favorites by **Heartsong Presents** readers. *Texas Rose* is the series book to *Texas Honor* and will soon be followed by *Texas Lady* and *Texas Angel*. A portion of the earnings from her writing goes to Christian Blind Mission, International. You may visit Debra on the world wide web at www.get-set.com/debrawhitesmith.

Books by Debra White Smith

HEARTSONG PRESENTS
HP237—The Neighbor
HP284—Texas Honor

Texas Rose

Debra White Smith

Heartsong Presents

Dedicated to my sister, Rebecca White.

A note from the author:
I love to hear from my readers! You may correspond with me by writing: **Debra White Smith**
Author Relations
PO Box 719
Uhrichsville, OH 44683

ISBN 1-57748-620-X

TEXAS ROSE

All of the characters and events in this book are fictitious. Any resemblance to actual persons, living or dead, or to actual events is purely coincidental.

Cover illustration by Lisa Peruchini.

PRINTED IN THE U.S.A.

prologue

(Taken from *Texas Honor*, Heartsong Presents # 284)

Barely hearing Kate's nervous chatter, Travis stared across the stagnant gray pond by which they had taken their afternoon meal. Before their picnic, he had briefly held Kate, had kissed her soft, rose-scented cheek, had looked deeply into her eyes. She told him she came simply because she missed him. But sadly enough, Travis felt no emotional tug. Sure, he felt sorry for Kate. She had, after all, lost one fiancé to death. And now, as the man responsible for that death, Travis was repaying her loyalty with betrayal. The whole thing was not fair.

Travis had taken something very precious from Kate and he was honor bound to repay her. And repay her he would, with a lifetime of devotion. Despite his heart's desire, though, despite his turbulent longings, he would keep his promise to Kate. Even if Travis couldn't control his wayward heart, he could control his choices.

Once Travis left, once he returned to El Paso, he hoped. . . he prayed he would forget about Rachel. Perhaps her memory would fade in the face of his new life with Kate. Perhaps Kate would bear him a child. Perhaps Travis would learn to love Kate with the same passion that Rachel awakened in him. Perhaps. . .perhaps. . .perhaps. How often would he "perhaps" before he realized the indelible impression that Rachel had left on his memory would never fade?

Sighing, he scrutinized the clump of cedars on the opposite bank. Travis felt as if a giant chain encompassed his heart, enslaving his soul to an unforgiving burden.

"You're in love with her, aren't you?" Kate's sudden question exploded into his musings.

Speechless, Travis stared into Kate's downcast eyes, creamy cheeks, and rosy lips. "What? Who?" he sputtered, not expecting Kate to ever suspect his love for Rachel, and especially not after mere hours in his and Rachel's company. Was he *that* obvious?

"You don't have to pretend, Travis." She looked up from the fried chicken and potato salad and lemonade to peer into his eyes, her own eyes the sad orbs of a lone owl, too wise for comfort. "I saw the way she looked at you. . .us when you introduced her. Then, when you left for the picnic, she watched us drive away."

Kate toyed with the red velvet reticule lying in her lap, her elegant neck and head like the melancholic droop of a weeping lily. She rushed on as if the words, left too long on her tongue, would cause unbearable pain. "I don't think she knew I saw her, but she was crying, and. . .and then there was that. . .that episode that Mr. Lionel and I stumbled onto which you never. . .never explained." Here, Kate halted as if to incite him to please expound on her final subject.

Swallowing against a throat tightening in accusation, Travis had never been so speechless. Silently he resumed his spot on the picnic blanket. Educated in the classics, an expert orator, a student of the law, and he could find no words to deny or acknowledge her claim. Instead, he looked helplessly into her eyes brimming with tears and reached to touch the dark tendril of hair escaping its restraint. How, oh how, had life become so complicated?

"You are the most beautiful woman I ever met, Kate. I—"

"But I'm not Rachel." Pressing the tips of her trembling, gloved fingers against unsteady lips, Kate held his gaze, her hazel eyes begging him to refute her words.

But he could not. "I'm so sorry," he breathed, taking in the smells of dried grass and earth and Kate's rose perfume. "I didn't mean. . .I didn't intend. . .I never wanted to hurt you. I—" A compulsive swallow.

"Were you even going to tell me?" she asked through a haze of tears. "Or were you just going to. . .to pretend and then marry me anyway?"

Blinking, Travis marveled at her perception.

"Why?" she demanded, her fists tightened in angry knots.

"Because. . .I couldn't, I won't abandon you, not after all that's happened."

"What do you mean, 'All that's happened?' What are you talking about?" The questions fell between them like a stifling pall. Questions that Travis didn't want to answer.

As he held her challenging gaze, autumn's cool breeze scampered across the brittle grass to tease Kate's hair and lace collar then mock him in accusing whispers. God knew Travis didn't want to hurt her any more than he had already hurt her. But Travis sensed that Kate Lowell would expect him to reveal the whole truth.

"You're talking about Zachary. . .about his death, aren't you?"

More silence.

"Why did you propose to me, Travis?"

He gazed toward a lone, gray fish that flipped its tail against the pond's smooth surface. "Kate. . ." he began, wishing to remove the note of pain in her voice, wishing she would accept his devotion without questions. Another glance her way and Travis knew he must reveal his heart. "I loved. . .love you, but I also felt. . .feel responsible for you because of Zach. . ." A choke, misty eyes, and his mind replayed that horrible morning when he had witnessed his best friend's demise. The pepperbox, that defective little pistol with all its barrels. Travis would have never let Zach shoot it if he'd known it was going to backfire and kill him.

"But it wasn't your fault!"

"Yes, it was. . .it was. You, yourself, called me a murderer," he groaned as an agony ripped through his soul, heaving like a storm-tortured ocean. Then came the tears that he had refused to release since Zach's death. Tears that could no longer be imprisoned in his distressed heart.

"But I–I. . ." And she was at his side, gripping his arm. "I didn't mean it. You know I didn't mean it. I was over-reacting. I. . .that was right after you came and told me that. . .that he was. . .was dead. . .that. . .that you had killed him. I didn't mean it," she said again, her voice cracking on a new sob.

"I didn't want him to die." Wrapping his arms around her, Travis buried his head in the rose-scented locks of her hair, and the barrier around his emotions collapsed, leaving him the shaking victim of overdue grief. "It was that pepperbox. . .that defective pepperbox. It misfired and the next thing I knew, Zachary was lying in a pool of his own blood."

"I know. . .I know," she whispered, stroking his hair like a mother comforting a child.

After several minutes of uncontrolled grief, Travis released a shuddering sigh and began to gain control of his emotions. He pulled away to grip her upper arms. "There's no way I can ever replace Zach, but at least I can try."

There, he had finally revealed the real reason he had proposed. And in the light of that truth, all glistening and penetrating, Travis also saw that he had never really loved Kate. Oh, he loved her as a brother might love his sister, but not as the woman of his heart. That place was reserved for Rachel.

With her face so close to him, with her tearful eyes boring twin points of doubt into his mind, Travis saw for the first time that Kate's feelings for him shrank in the shadow of her feelings for Zachary.

"Why did you agree to marry me?" he blurted, suddenly needing to know her reasons.

"Because. . .because. . .I. . ." Now it was her turn to flounder. "I needed someone so desperately," she rushed, "and. . . and I felt that you needed me, and. . .and I knew that after Zachary, after my love for him, that I would. . .that it wouldn't matter that. . . Then I grew to care so deeply for you, Travis. Don't think that I don't love you, because I do. As I told you in my letter, I have begun to depend on you so much that I have felt that I cannot live without you."

"And I love you, too," he muttered, kissing her forehead.

"But not the same way you love Rachel."

"And not the same way you loved Zach."

"No."

Reflective silence. The kind that reveals a truth, long hidden.

Standing, Travis walked through the scruffy grass and aimlessly kicked a loose rock into the pond's placid face. The silent moment hung about his shoulders. What would Kate do if they did not marry?

one

Dogwood, Texas
October 1885

"You misled me, Mr. Adams! You never once told me your son was an. . .an *Indian*." The petite blond stubbornly stared toward the empty train tracks, avoiding eye contact with the tall, bearded man standing nearby. "My Christian convictions simply will not allow me to tutor such a child!"

Kate Lowell turned her back on the arguing man and woman. Arranging her royal blue skirt, she lowered herself to the hard bench outside the train station's ticket office. She hoped to avoid further eavesdropping on the troubled pair, but wondered if that were possible, given their close proximity. Just a few days ago, Kate had come to Dogwood, Texas to visit her fiancé, Travis Campbell. She arrived in Dogwood an engaged woman. Now, she was returning home to El Paso and a future devoid of matrimony.

"How exactly do you perceive that my son's heritage goes against *your* Christian convictions?" the man demanded.

"The Good Book says we aren't to associate with–with things that are *dirty*, and. . .and. . ."

Forgetting all propriety, Kate's head snapped up. She peered into the face of the bearded gentleman who appeared to be on the brink of losing all control. A red flush slowly crept up his neck toward his forehead. His dark eyes virtually shot bullets into the blond. His hands coiled and uncoiled like twin cobras ready to assault their victims.

Kate's stomach churned with the obvious emotions pouring from the man. Her gloved hands, chilled with autumn's breeze, trembled when she recognized the petite blond's attitude. Kate's own mother recently displayed this same attitude when a poor Tigua Indian girl asked Kate for a few coins.

"Ignore her," Kate's mother insisted. "You'll only contribute to the problem. She needs to get a job."

But who would hire her? Kate wanted to ask. The only place the unfortunate creature could hope to find work would be in one of the dance halls or saloons or houses of prostitution that lined El Paso's main street. The sleepy little town of Kate's childhood was certainly not the El Paso of the present. The coming of the railroad had transformed the city in many ways, some of them for the better, some for the worse. Kate understood all too well that an orphaned Indian girl stood little chance for more than a life of hardship and early death. Kate's fingers had ached to reach into her reticule and give the unfortunate beggar all the money she carried. But her mother insisted, and Kate turned her back on the young girl. She blended in with the El Paso pedestrians, and Kate never saw her again.

But her image was emblazoned on Kate's mind. Every time she tried to pray, the Indian girl's forlorn face still tore at her heart. The girl's pleading eyes pierced her soul when she attended church alongside El Paso's prominent citizens. Many of them proudly wore their Christianity like a new suit that mustn't be sullied with those who participated in the vices now so prominent in town.

What would the bearded stranger think if he knew I had refused to help a girl who shared his son's heritage? Kate pondered. Presently, the man seemed so busy grappling with self-control that he had few other concerns. At last, he turned away from the blond and stomped toward a farm wagon harnessed to a black gelding.

"Drew! Let's go!" he snapped as he boarded the wagon. A dark-haired, dark-eyed lad ran toward the wagon from across the street. He looked about fourteen years old—all legs and arms. The boy clambered into the wagon with a question on his lips. The man cast a troubled glance toward the haughty, erect woman then produced a soft smile for his son. "She wasn't the right one," he said.

As the curious lad peered around his father toward the blond, Kate was thankful he had obviously missed the woman's tirade. Drew's skin, the color of coffee mixed with heavy cream, his high cheekbones, and prominent nose, all spoke strongly of his mixed heritage.

The boy needs a tutor. Mr. Adams' plight echoed in Kate's mind as a westward bound train whistled in the distance. Kate looked toward the east to see the steam engine's pillar of smoke billowing atop the autumn-hued trees. The 10:40 would soon arrive to carry Kate back to El Paso—back to the place where nothing awaited her— nothing but an empty future and rounds of meaningless social activities.

The boy needs a tutor. Kate had served as her niece's tutor last year when the dear girl had been so sick. She glanced toward the man and his son. Mr. Adams picked up the reins and tapped them against the horse's back. The young Indian girl in the streets of El Paso trailed through her mind once more. As her thoughts raced, Kate worried the brown train ticket, which she clutched like a lifeline.

The boy needs a tutor. Why not you? The thought was a whisper in her spirit, a nuance in her soul. Nonetheless, it sent her heart racing with possibilities. She started to jump up, but stopped herself. Kate Lowell had never made an impulsive decision in her life. Her mother trained her from birth to exude an aura of reserved dignity. "There is simply no room for impulsiveness among the well-bred and upper class," she could hear her mother say.

But apparently, neither was there room for compassion or charity. Could it be that God was giving Kate a second chance? She had refused to help once before; could she dare refuse again?

Mr. Adams turned the horse toward the rutted street.

Kate jumped up, her legs quaking beneath her. "Excuse me. Sir!" she called, rushing toward the departing wagon.

The man continued his journey.

"Excuse me!" Kate yelled again. She had never raised her voice in public before. Now she felt the gaze of every waiting passenger penetrating her back. But the haunted eyes of the Indian girl in El Paso proved a stronger motivator.

Still, the man didn't acknowledge her call.

With renewed determination, Kate clamped her plumed hat down with one hand and lifted her skirt with the other. She ran off the wooded walkway and onto the dried grass, attempting once more to gain the man's attention. "Mr. Adams!" she called. "Please, wait!"

He abruptly pulled on the horse's reins and turned around, his face dark with anger. Kate didn't let his expression stop her. *The boy needs a tutor.* By the time she stood beside the wagon, Mr. Adams observed her with surprise. Kate received the distinct impression that he thought the blond had been calling him.

Now that his attention was hers, Kate was immediately plagued with doubts. Had she taken leave of all her senses? She had never even seen Mr. Adams until minutes before. Nervously, she eyed his revolver, ensconced in its holster. The man might be a gunfighter or a scoundrel at large. But, as Kate peered up into soft brown eyes that reflected a deep compassion, she knew at once that Mr. Adams could never be an evil man.

"Was there something you needed of me, Ma'am?" he asked in the soft voice of a cultured gentleman. A voice that strongly contrasted with the angry tones he used with the blond. A voice that didn't match his worn denim shirt, scruffy boots, and the dusty wooden wagon. He gracefully removed his hat to reveal a shock of light brown hair, a shade fairer than his beard and brows. Kate recognized the traces of upper society in his every move. Who was this gracious gentleman, dressed as a farmer? And what was he doing in a small east Texas town?

Kate strained to breathe against her corset's snug fit. "Did I understand you to say that you are looking for a tutor for your son?"

"Yes." Mr. Adams cast a troubled glance toward the train tracks where the 10:40 hissed to a stop with metal screeching against metal.

"It's possible that I might be interested in the position," Kate supplied.

Mr. Adams' brows rose sharply. His son leaned forward to scrutinize her with questioning, dark eyes. Suddenly, Kate felt like a heifer under examination on the auction block. Adams briefly glanced at Kate's tailor-made traveling frock and the ivory brooch pinned to her lapel.

"While the position is honorable, Miss. . ."

"Miss Kate Lowell," Kate said firmly, sounding much more self-confident than she felt.

"Miss Lowell." A spark of recognition registered in the stranger's eyes—eyes surrounded by tanned lines that attested to long hours in the sun.

Kate wondered how he could possibly know her.

"I am McCall Adams, and this is my son, Drew."

"Pleased to meet you."

Drew produced a ready smile as the horse shifted restlessly from one hoof to another.

"While I appreciate your interest, I cannot imagine the position would in any way pay enough to support your current standard of—"

"This has nothing to do with money, " Kate interrupted. She glanced over her shoulder toward the train and hoped it would maintain an appropriately long layover—long enough for her to make a decision.

"Oh?" Mr. Adams said, his kind brown eyes assuming a hint of surprise.

If only Adams could have felt her compassion for that unfortunate Indian girl. If only he could sense her sensitivity to God's will or her anguish over the choice of staying in Dogwood rather than returning to the safety of home and family. "There are things more precious than money," she answered.

"Well, in that case, I think perhaps we should discuss the situation."

"Yes, that would be nice."

"Can you meet me in about twenty minutes at the cafe on the corner?" He pointed toward an eating establishment with "Dotty's" painted in red across the large front window.

"I will make arrangements for Drew to visit with a friend while you and I discuss the position."

"Yes. Yes. That will be fine. Thank you."

"And thank you," he returned, a wisp of relief teasing the corners of his mouth.

⁂

How could Kate have failed to notice just how handsome Mr. Adams actually was? Perhaps the distraction of making such a quick decision had clouded her thoughts. Furthermore, the hurried moments when she re-checked into the hotel and rushed to Dotty's didn't allow her time to reflect on the man's appearance. But as they settled into the straight-backed chairs at the homey eating establishment, Kate, at long last, realized what she had initially failed to recognize. With Mr. Adams' contemplative gaze on her, she was taken aback by the strong angles of his square jaw, the aristocratic lines of his straight nose. Once again, she peered into eyes full of compassion and something else, something Kate recognized all too well. Pain.

"I can't imagine that you didn't overhear the whole conversation at the train station between Miss Pimberly and me."

"Yes, I heard." Kate chose to look across the cheerful room at the collection of rough oak tables covered with red checked cloths, at the bare pine walls, at the half-opened kitchen door—at anything other than Mr. Adams. Had she been thinking clearly when she agreed to this meeting? Her mother would be aghast, to say the least. But her mother wasn't present, and Kate was now a young woman—almost twenty-three. She could make her own decisions.

"Does it not bother you that my son is of mixed heritage?" he asked in a deceptively soft voice that riveted Kate's attention.

"Not in the least."

Mr. Adams' guarded eyes softened to reveal an unconditional love for Drew. "He's all I've got," he rasped. "My wife died soon after she bore him. And when I hear someone say something like. . .like. . ." His hands curled on the table.

Once more, Kate saw the pain in his eyes. A pain that went deep. A pain that touched her heart of hearts. Kate knew that kind of pain. Intimately. She understood the agony of losing that special person, the one most beloved.

Zachary. Zachary. Zachary. His memory echoed within her soul like tormenting midnight thunder. Would she ever free herself from him?

Already, she felt a kindred spirit with this stranger, a common understanding of what it means to have loved and lost. Suddenly, the feeling scared her beyond reason. Why in the name of common sense had she chased him down and expressed an interest in the tutoring position? Was this encounter indeed of God? Or, was it nothing but a product of her own guilt over not helping the girl in El Paso?

"I'm a horse breeder. I own a farm three miles east of Dogwood. If you agree to the tutoring position, we have a schoolroom set up in our summer kitchen there at the homestead. It has everything you would need to facilitate your teaching.

"Drew is a good boy," Mr. Adams continued as the plump waitress placed aromatic coffee and homemade cinnamon rolls on the table before them. "He is intelligent and strong and should give you very little trouble.

"From what I understand, you have been educated at an eastern university? Am I correct?"

Kate blinked in amazement. How did Mr. Adams know

of her background? "Yes. You're right. I—how did you know about me?"

"This is a small town," he supplied with a slight smile. "You can't stay here two days without the whole place humming with every detail of your life. I also have heard that you live in El Paso and were here to visit an. . . acquaintance."

"I see," Kate said as her face warmed. He must be referring to her broken engagement with Travis Campbell. The very idea that this man would bring up something so intensely personal left her astounded. Had living in a small country town completely removed all vestiges of propriety from him? "I guess that means I'll know all your secrets by tomorrow," she snapped in defense.

"Don't count on it," he challenged. Kate felt the verbal slap as keenly as any physical one. Furthermore, his guarded, hostile expression warned her not to get any closer.

What could he be hiding that left him so wary? Some haunting mystery seemed to cloak his every feature.

Suddenly, Kate decided not to accept the tutoring position. Within the few minutes she had been in this man's presence, she felt as though she were being drawn into a tangled web of past pain and secrets of the heart. Kate's own wounds since losing Zachary were still gaping sores of agony. She was still unable to burden herself with the heartache of another.

Then she remembered that Indian girl in El Paso. Would those dark eyes never cease to haunt her? As that girl had needed money, Drew Adams, also, had a need. If Kate rejected Drew, she would be rejecting that poor beggar all over again. Thus, her thoughts vacillated from one wave to another like an unanchored ship in a tempestuous sea.

"I'm sorry," Mr. Adams said at last, a gentleman's smile tilting his lips. "I didn't mean to snap at you."

"Nor I, you," Kate returned, responding to his kind expression with an apologetic smile of her own. Despite her former pondering about Zachary, Kate could not deny her heart's stirring response to this man's smooth charm. She wondered how many women had lost their hearts without his ever knowing it. She also wondered if she should guard her own heart because of her tender feelings for Zachary.

"Excuse me, Mr. Adams," an attractive blond lady called from the doorway.

"Yes, Miss Alexander?" Mr. Adams replied, his brow furrowed in alarm. "What's the matter? I left Drew with you and Dr. Engle—"

"The doctor sent me for you. There's a terrible altercation with Eugene Wilcox's son in the street. Dr. Engle seems to think you better stop it before Eugene finds out."

Mr. Adams stood, his chair toppling behind him. "Please excuse me," he stated curtly as he ran toward the doorway.

two

McCall raced down the boardwalk toward the circle of shouting boys who had congregated on the dusty street in front of Dr. Engle's office. The sounds of intermittent punches and grunts mingled with juvenile yelling. Over the din, Dr. Engle's voice shouted, "Stop it! You two, stop it now!"

In a matter of seconds, McCall broke through the rowdy ring of boys to see his son, covered in dirt and his mouth bleeding. The young Adams straddled the blond Calvin Wilcox, who wriggled face-down beneath Drew's weight. Gritting his teeth, McCall grabbed his son under the arms and dragged him off his adversary. Calvin, his faded overalls soiled with dirt and blood, gasped for air.

"Calvin's the one who started it. I saw the whole thing," Dr. Engle growled as he glared at the wiry bully. Just then, Calvin rolled over, jumped to his feet, and dove head-long toward Drew's midsection.

McCall, still gripping his son, sidestepped Calvin. His move sent Calvin hurling into the travel-hardened road. Calvin sputtered against a mouthful of dirt as he scrambled to regain his footing.

The huffing, angry Drew struggled against McCall's grasp. "Don't you ever jump me like that again, Calvin Wilcox," he yelled. "I didn't do one thing to you! You. . . you. . ."

"What's goin' on here?" an angry bear-like voice

boomed from down the street.

"That's Calvin's father." Dr. Engle's nurse, Magnolia Alexander, worriedly gazed down the street.

"He's nothin' but trouble," Dr. Engle said urgently. "You two need to get out of here. *Now*." The graying Dr. Engle had been a second father to McCall, a grandfather to Drew. From the moment McCall bought the horse farm thirteen years ago, the doctor had been a mainstay while the younger man raised his adopted son. Dr. Engle, the only person in Dogwood who knew the story behind Drew's parentage, had recommended an excellent nanny who was not a gossip. Thus, McCall was able to guard his and Drew's privacy. At this point, Drew himself didn't even know the whole story of his parentage.

McCall dragged the flailing Drew toward their wagon, parked near Dotty's. "I'm gonna beat the stuffin' out of that Calvin Wilcox," Drew protested.

"Looks like you already have to me," McCall said sarcastically. With a grunt, he hefted Drew onto the bags of flour, sugar, and cornmeal in the back of the wagon.

Drew sat up.

His father shoved him back down. "Stay flat, and don't get up until I say you can. You've already caused enough of a scene. The less Eugene Wilcox sees of you, the better."

"I didn't cause a scene," Drew said, his bleeding bottom lip stubbornly set. "Calvin did. I was just defending myself."

"We're gonna get you for this!" Eugene Wilcox bellowed from the crowd of boys.

McCall climbed onto the bench seat and glanced over his shoulder to see Eugene holding a sagging Calvin, nose bleeding, eyes swollen. Grinding his teeth, McCall released the wagon's brake and snapped the reins over the horse's back. He looked toward Dotty's to see Kate forlornly staring at him from the boardwalk. With a groan, McCall realized he had completely forgotten about the new tutor. What should he do?

Spontaneously, he pulled the horse to a halt and jumped from the wagon. Without preamble, he scooped the petite Miss Lowell into his arms.

"Oh, *please* Mr. Adams. What are you *thinking*?" she protested, while firmly gripping her oversized, plumed hat.

"I'm thinking you and I need to talk some more, and Drew and I need to get out of town as fast as we can," he said, plopping her onto the wagon seat.

She landed with a muffled gasp.

Her rose perfume's delicate fragrance clung to his denim shirt, and McCall tried to produce a gentlemanly smile. He was certain he came closer to a grimace. With the sound of Eugene Wilcox's unedited expletives in their wake, McCall once more cracked the reins over the ebony gelding's haunches and the wagon jerked.

"Mr. Adams, I find this *highly* unsuitable," Miss Lowell protested nervously as the buggy jarred over the ruts formed during the last rainstorm. "I hardly know you. Please sir, I think it would be much better if you would just allow me to return to my hotel room, and—"

"Of course," McCall said over the sound of the horses pounding hooves. "I agree with all you've said. And you'll have to forgive me. Under normal circumstances, I would have never behaved so. But given my son's recent. . .escapade, I think it would be much better for me to avoid town for a couple of weeks." McCall paused to allow Miss Lowell to contemplate the aspects of Drew's parentage, which could easily guarantee a conviction, even in the face of his innocence.

"You will agree that the two of us need to discuss the arrangements for your tutoring position. I could hardly have left you waiting at the hotel indefinitely. And given the mood of Eugene Wilcox, I could hardly have taken the time to assist you into the buggy properly." McCall produced a smile, hoping to assure the beautiful young woman that he, in no way, intended to harm her. But the trembling, uncertain twist of her lips left him feeling like a cad.

As they sped from the streets of Dogwood and down the wooded lane to his farm, McCall wondered what had possessed him to scoop this immaculate lady into his arms and plop her onto the wagon seat. Had the situation truly called for such cavalier action? Or had McCall simply responded to the impulse that had urged him to get closer to Kate Lowell from the moment she sat across from him at Dotty's? If he were completely honest with himself, he would admit that she was the first woman he had met since Melody's death who awakened more than a passing interest. Something in Kate Lowell's eyes hinted that the two of them shared a similar way of thought. But despite the attraction he felt for her, McCall knew he could never be unfaithful to the memory of his Melody.

"Exactly how do you propose that I return to the hotel? I *cannot* stay at your farm," Miss Lowell stated firmly.

"Of course not. Dr. Engle will come out later to check on Drew. You can go back into town with him." McCall said, concentrating on the hardened path before him.

"You are certain the doctor will pay a visit?"

"Absolutely. He'll want to take a look at Drew's lip. He's like a second father to me."

"Well, in that case. . ."

McCall felt Kate relaxing and was relieved that she no longer worried about her predicament.

The thick, barren woods produced a wall on each side of the lane, shading them from the bright autumn sunshine. As McCall slowed the horse's rapid pace, the piney forest's cool, earthy smell seemed to awaken the common sense that Miss Lowell's blatant beauty had momentarily defused. McCall made a personal vow, then and there, to never make eye contact again with his son's tutor. The effect practically mesmerized him. He had been a man alone too long, and she was simply too lovely for her own good.

"Can I sit up now, Dad?" Drew asked from behind.

"Sure, son."

"Hi!" Drew exclaimed as he pulled himself onto the seat beside his new teacher. "I'm Drew." He produced a swollen smile that made McCall want to groan. Was he so wise to hire such a pretty lady for his son's educator?

But you don't have a choice. The reality of their desperate situation settled around McCall's neck like a harness on a weary plow horse. He really didn't have a choice. Up until recently, McCall had tutored Drew. But the cares of the ranch pulled McCall away from Drew's increasing educational demands. Now, he desperately needed a tutor. It was out of the question for Drew to attend school in town. Today's fight with Calvin Wilcox proved just how unaccepting the townspeople were of Drew. McCall simply wasn't ready to see his son live through the misery that one human being can force upon another because of blind prejudice.

As a last resort, McCall had placed an ad for a tutor in the Dallas paper, hoping to attract some applicants who were open-minded enough to willingly tutor a child of Drew's heritage. Of all the applicants, only Miss Pimberly had obtained a college education, one of McCall's definite requirements. When she refused, McCall had despaired of ever hiring a tutor. But to have Miss Lowell appear from nowhere following Miss Pimberly's despicable rejection. . . the likelihood of such an occurrence being anything more than divine providence surpassed McCall's comprehension. *Miss Kate Lowell must be an answer to my many prayers.*

McCall simply hoped he understood all of God's motives. Something within him cringed at the thought of fully releasing his hold on Melody, even for God. True, she had been gone fourteen years, but she still lived in McCall's heart. The thought of betraying her memory filled him with nothing but guilt. He fervently hoped that God wasn't placing the stunning Miss Lowell into his life for a purpose other than tutoring Drew. Anything more than an employer/employee relationship left McCall wanting to run in the other direction.

However, he could not deny that the woman sitting next to him did appeal to his masculinity. He repeated the vow to never again make eye contact with her. Once McCall showed her the schoolroom and observed her bonding with Drew, he would confirm his wish to hire her. From that point forward, he would maintain his distance, at all costs—for Melody.

੨

Eugene Wilcox watched as McCall Adams rode out of town with that woman beside him. He hadn't seen where that stinkin' Indian boy had gone, but Eugene would bet his last steer that Drew Adams was lying in the back of the wagon, like the lowlife coward he was. He turned to his son, who held his right wrist and whimpered and moaned like a chewed-up mutt. Calvin's friends, who moments ago cheered for him, now snickered under their breath as they went in search of excitement elsewhere.

"Get in the wagon," Eugene growled, pushing Calvin toward their horse and wagon, tethered across the street. "How many times have I told you not to get into a fight you can't win?"

"I didn't have no choice," Calvin whined. "That Injun boy tripped me, and I had to defend myself."

"He's lying!" Dr. Engle called. "He's the one who started it. He jumped Drew from behind for no reason. I saw the whole thing myself."

Hiking up his baggy work pants, the wiry Eugene turned toward the doctor's establishment, which served as both his home and office. He looked the elderly man square in the eyes and dared him to refute his next words. "I believe my son. And you need to stay out of this."

"There's nothing to stay out of. It's over." The doctor pushed up his wire-rimmed spectacles as that saucy nurse of his nodded her agreement. "And you'll be wise to drop the whole thing."

"I'll drop it when that stinkin' Injun pays for humiliatin' Calvin in front of his friends." For added emphasis, Eugene spit a stream of sweet tobacco juice onto the sandy road.

"Calvin is the one who humiliated himself when he jumped Drew from behind. That's no way for a young man to act. Calvin deserved every punch he got."

"Yes. He's right," Magnolia added.

The thin Eugene, now rigid with anger, doubled his fists

and glared at the interfering doctor and his nurse. "I didn't ask for no report from you! I know my son. And I know those stinkin' Injuns. There ain't a one of 'em alive who's worth his keep!"

Wilcox observed at Dr. Engle as he clamped his lips together in that uppity way of his. The man acted like he knew everything. Truth of the matter, Eugene thought he knew far more about Indians than that haughty doctor ever would. His grandpa had told him story after story of the way those Cherokees had tried to steal everything from chickens to Wilcox women. Eugene grew up hating Indians. He still hated Indians. And he would make doubly certain that Indian of McCall Adams' suffered for beating up Calvin.

Deciding to ignore Dr. Engle, Eugene grabbed Calvin's arm and marched toward their worn wagon. He'd get the boy home and wear him out for letting the likes of an Indian beat him up.

"Don't go so fast, Pa," Calvin whined, hobbling beside him.

"Just get in the wagon," Eugene demanded. "I'm just hopin' no one I know saw you get whipped. It's a shame and disgrace!"

Calvin, still nursing his right wrist, struggled to pull himself into the wagon.

Eugene gave him a quick shove, and the boy stumbled forward to collapse onto the seat.

"I think I need to take a look at Calvin's wrist," Dr. Engle said from behind.

New rage twisting his gut, Eugene spun and grabbed a handful of Dr. Engle's woolen shirt in his callused fist. "Stay out of our business," he growled, only inches from the physician's wrinkled face.

"When I see someone who has an injured wrist, it's my business!" the doctor growled.

Eugene couldn't believe the pluck of the old man. Didn't Dr. Engle know Eugene could knock him flat with one blow? "I'll tend to my boy. If he needs doctorin', I'll take care of it!"

The doctor looked past Eugene, toward Calvin. "Tell your mother I'm here, if you need me."

Eugene firmly shoved the doctor away from the wagon, untethered the horse, crawled up to the bench, and snapped the reins over the dappled mare's back. If it took him a solid year, he'd see that sorry Drew Adams punished for what happened today.

He hadn't seen Drew more than a dozen times in the last decade. Drew and his pa stayed pretty much to themselves. But the whole town knew the boy's ma must have been nothing more than a rotten squaw. What a clean white man like McCall Adams would have ever wanted with a squaw went beyond Eugene's understanding. As he encouraged his tired mare out of town and down the tree-lined dirt road, Eugene ground his teeth and determined to see the day when McCall and Drew would both wish they had never moved to these parts.

three

Two weeks after accepting her teaching assignment, Kate Lowell stood gazing out her hotel window across the rolling hills, now ablaze with autumn's splendor. Occasionally, she looked up the busy, rutted streets for the familiar sight of Dr. Engle's black, hooded buggy. As Mr. Adams had predicted, the doctor did indeed pay a visit to check on Drew the evening of his unfortunate encounter with Calvin. Then, the kind physician had escorted Kate back to the hotel and provided transportation to and from the horse farm every school day since. Dr. Engle had agreed with Mr. Adams that he should avoid town indefinitely due to Eugene Wilcox's livid temper.

Kate closed her eyes and reflected over the last two weeks. She hadn't seen Mr. Adams more than three times. During those few occasions, he had remained aloof and seemed to look past her rather than at her. Kate had the disturbing impression that the man was taking extra pains to ignore her.

Drew, on the other hand, did nothing but look at her. Kate sensed, almost from the beginning, that the boy held an immediate fancy for her and she responded in an appropriately cool and professional manner. The handsome lad was nothing short of brilliant, far above his age in intellectual capacity and achievements. Kate felt a deep sense of satisfaction in knowing that she opened new doors to Drew's knowledge. At long last, thoughts of the

Indian girl from the streets of El Paso were put to rest. However, new thoughts, just as disturbing, plagued her. She was overcome with curiosity about McCall Adams and his former wife. Strangely, Drew didn't favor his father in the least.

A soft tap at her door arrested her reverie. "Miss Lowell?" a hesitant feminine voice called.

Kate walked across the faded floral rug and opened her door to the smiling face of the hotel owner's timid, plain daughter. "Yes?" Kate asked.

"There's a Mr. Adams waiting for you downstairs," the girl said, and with a quick curtsy, she was gone.

Kate compulsively gripped the doorknob as her throat tightened. Thoughts of sitting next to Mr. Adams during the thirty-minute ride to the horse farm left Kate with a multitude of tremors flitting up and down her spine. *Nonsense*, Kate scolded herself. *You're being unreasonable,* she thought as she retrieved her black velvet reticule from the poster bed's quilted coverlet. The man had no interest in her whatsoever, as attested by his obviously ignoring her the last two weeks. He had even paid her by sending an envelope with Drew that held her bi-weekly salary of twenty dollars. As she stepped into the hallway, Kate decided she would simply treat the father in the same manner she treated the son—with the same cool dignity her mother had long since taught her.

Schooling her features into a pleasant mask, Kate descended the flight of steps at the end of the musty, narrow hallway. She saw Mr. Adams long before he saw her. McCall leaned against the modest reception desk, chatting with the hotel's plump owner. Not quite understanding her motive, Kate paused halfway down the steps to examine the tall, lean man. The man of many walls. The man of shadowed corridors.

What dreadful pain from his past caused him to shut out the world? Essentially, that was what he had done. He had shut out everyone, except Drew, of course, and Dr. Engle. He didn't even attend Sunday services, although Kate knew beyond a doubt that the Lord was vitally important to him. The fact that he had emphatically requested that Kate teach Drew from the Word of God underscored his belief in a Holy Creator. Kate was momentarily overcome with a raging curiosity about her employer, who carried himself like a handsome prince. A nagging little voice made her wonder what it would feel like to have his strong arms wrapped around her.

Kate's face heated at the very thought, and much to her dismay, Mr. Adams looked straight at her. His brow quirked momentarily. His nostrils flared. And under his unwavering gaze, Kate sensed that he knew she had been examining him. Her hands produced an annoying film of sweat. Her legs trembled. Her stomach clenched into a tight knot. Then, something she hadn't felt since before Zachary's death swept through her soul—the fire of attraction. Never had she known such an attraction for Travis Campbell, her former fiancé. Kate thought she would never feel it again. Never, for anyone except her beloved Zachary.

Oh, Lord, help me! Kate pleaded. She should board the next train to El Paso and leave this town, leave McCall Adams' web of mystery, which daily seemed to enclose her all the tighter.

As their gaze lengthened, she was further dismayed to see reflections of her own turbulent emotions shimmering in the depths of McCall's eyes. The unwavering attraction. The dismay. The urge to bolt. Her stomach lurched, and Kate wondered if his avoiding her stemmed from an intent to escape such an encounter as this. *Why did you ever agree to this tutoring position,* she questioned herself.

But which was better? Life in El Paso, trapped in a round of meaningless social activities and haunted by that poor Indian girl—or being here, in this tiny east Texas town, pouring herself into a worthy occupation?

At long last, she forced herself to look down and slowly descend the stairs. On the last step, the heel of Kate's ankle boot tangled in the hem of her gingham dress. She had arranged for it to be made just a few days earlier. Nothing in her trunk seemed appropriate attire for a tutor on a horse farm, but the new dress was proving her tormentor. She hadn't realized until this morning that it was a bit too long for her. Now, she was forever tripping over the skirt. Feeling as if she were in a dream, Kate stumbled forward, but her firm grip on the banister stopped her fall.

She felt Mr. Adams at her side before she saw him. His steady hand on her elbow did nothing but increase her lack of equilibrium *and* her pulse.

"Are you all right?" he asked softly.

"Yes, fine. I'm fine. Thank you," Kate squeaked out, refusing to look at him.

"The buggy is out front. I thought you might prefer it to the wagon."

"Yes. That's thoughtful of you," she supplied, stubbornly keeping her focus on the lobby's faded floral rug, a larger version of the one in her room. All of Dogwood's quaint establishments paled in comparison to some of the ornate structures in the east where Kate had attended university or even those in El Paso. Nonetheless, Kate had grown increasingly fond of the friendly atmosphere that Dogwood offered. The simplicity of its people, their amiability and charm, only added to Kate's growing fancy for the town.

However, Kate could not deny that a dark, dark streak of something sinister and evil slithered through the streets of this charming community. There was a reason Dr. Engle had been emphatic about McCall and Drew staying out of town for awhile. There was a reason Mr. Adams was forced to hire a tutor. Kate could never deny the ugly truth, no matter how delightful the residents appeared.

Silently, McCall assisted Kate into the hooded buggy, which looked a lot like Dr. Engle's. Silently, he took the seat beside her. Silently, they began the short journey toward the horse farm and another day of schoolwork for Drew. The wordlessness only added to Kate's overwrought emotions. Her stomach twisted in nervous nausea.

"I shall escort you back and forth to town from now on," McCall said, his breath a cloudy mist in the cold, morning air.

Any reply stuck in Kate's throat. She shivered with the breeze as the cantering mare pulled them away from Dogwood and down the familiar, tree-lined lane. Impulsively, she tugged her woolen, black cape closer around her shoulders.

"Are you cold?" McCall asked.

Kate, feeling his gaze on her, shook her head. "I'm f–f–fine," she stuttered in reply, her teeth chattering.

"You *are* cold." He pulled the chestnut horse to a halt, and with one swift motion, removed his coarse, leather jacket. "Here."

Kate attempted a protest, only to have him brush aside

her resistance. "This is the coldest morning we've had yet," he said. "And I forgot to bring any kind of quilt. We can't have you catching cold."

The heavy coat, several times too large for Kate, draped around her shoulders, seeping warmth into her. Warmth, and the smells of well-groomed horses. The smells of a man who spent many hours outdoors. "Thanks," she said, glancing up with a shy smile.

She should have never made that mistake. For that quick glance into McCall Adams' soft brown eyes turned into a long gaze, fraught with admiration.

❧

For two weeks, McCall had watched her. For two weeks, he had felt as if he were being drawn to Miss Lowell like a moth, fatefully flirting with a candle's flame. *God help me, she's beautiful. Too beautiful*, he mused, as their gaze lengthened. He had thought. . .McCall honestly had thought he could escort her to and from the farm and maintain his distance. Had he been fooling himself?

He wanted to kiss her. Here. Now. He wanted to feel her in his arms.

But those feelings were far, far, far from appropriate. Miss Kate Lowell was truly a proper lady. McCall, always the gentleman, would never violate the laws of propriety. Never. No matter how much his heart urged him to respond.

Plus, there was Melody. How could he have forgotten her? He hadn't thought of her all morning. The realization made him mentally scold himself with a stream of invectives. How could he forget the woman who had borne Drew? How could he forget the pain she had endured? Was he so weak that one pretty face swept aside all former loyalty to the memory of his wife?

Nonetheless, like a man under the hypnotic gaze of a sorceress, these thoughts immediately blurred as he basked under the spell of Kate's lovely, hazel eyes. Eyes much wiser than her years. Eyes that testified to seeing substantial pain. Eyes that seemed to peer into his very soul and understand McCall's own agony. No one except his grandfather and Dr. Engle had ever offered that kind of understanding. Even McCall's own family turned from him in his hour of deepest need. Only McCall's relationship with Jesus Christ had stopped him from falling into the pits of despair.

Perhaps God put Kate Lowell into your life for more reasons than tutoring. The thought echoed disturbingly as McCall continued to helplessly gaze into her limpid eyes. With the forest full of birds, cheerfully singing about starting their day, McCall wondered why God would fling him into the throws of a romance. Didn't the Lord know McCall wasn't ready for any kind of relationship? He still clung to Melody. His dear, sweet Melody. She may be gone from the earth but certainly not from McCall's heart.

At long last, Miss Lowell tore her gaze from his and looked at her hands, tightly clasped in her lap. "Don't–don't you think we sh–should continue our j–journey?" she rasped, turning her attention toward the woods.

"Certainly," McCall barked. Disgusted with his own reactions, he gripped the reins and slapped them against the horse's haunches.

Within half an hour, their reticent, strained journey ended. McCall stopped the carriage next to the massive, hay-strewn barn, which sat close to the log cabin he built with his own hands thirteen years before. The vast expanse of rolling, east Texas hills, ablaze with autumn, seemed to close in on him and only intensified his need to distance himself from the lovely tutor.

McCall couldn't help but notice the swiftness with which Miss Lowell disembarked the carriage. She didn't even tarry to wait for his assistance. That was quite all right with him. The fewer encounters they shared, the better. Furthermore, McCall would soon ask his hired hand, Bob Mosely, to provide transportation for Miss Lowell to and from the farm. McCall could not risk another experience like this morning's. His heart was in no way ready to be involved with a woman, regardless of God's plans.

≈

Kate rushed toward the summer kitchen, her heart pounding so furiously she could hardly catch her breath. With a muffled sob, she stumbled into the log structure, full of shadows, and collapsed at the rough-hewn, pine table where she taught Drew. Fortunately Drew was not present and Kate seized the opportunity to regain her composure.

During those heavy moments when she and McCall Adams stared into each other's eyes, Kate wanted so much more from her employer than a mere friendship. God help her, McCall might as well have kissed her. She felt nothing short of emotionally shattered from the incident. Though they had never even touched physically, their hearts had indeed touched. Did this signal the beginnings of love? If so, Kate should board the next train home. She was not ready, in any fashion, to commit to loving a man as she had once loved Zachary. Kate had experienced the consuming grief of a broken heart once. That was enough for a lifetime.

Pressing her lips together, she removed the dainty handkerchief from the hidden pocket in her blue gingham dress. She dabbled at her damp eyes and firmly pressed her lips together. She must focus on the task at hand and turn her mind from Mr. Adams' beseeching brown eyes. Otherwise, she would have no peace.

Determinedly, Kate squared her shoulders, took a deep breath, stood, and began rolling up and tying the oilcloth that covered the kitchen's numerous windows. With the bright autumn sunshine now streaming into the room, Kate lit only one lantern. She noticed the trace coals in the rock fireplace and wondered why Drew had not finished his list of chores, which included keeping the fire ablaze.

Where is Drew anyway? she mused, turning to look out one of the windows, toward the log cabin. But a glance toward the cabin meant another glimpse of Mr. Adams. Like a man on a mission, he briskly walked onto the long front porch, whipped open the door, and stepped into his home. Abruptly Kate whirled from the window, her heart pounding. Even the slightest glimpse of Mr. Adams brought to mind those tense moments when their spirits had touched.

Her hands trembling anew, Kate noticed a slip of paper in the spot where Drew normally sat. On it was a message scrawled in his familiar handwriting, a script that should belong to a grown man, not a fledgling boy. "I have gone for a walk. I will be back soon. Yours, Drew."

Kate tossed the note back onto the table. He had done it to her again. The third time in two weeks. But this time, not only had Drew disappeared before the day even started, he had also left without feeding the fire. Kate had refrained from mentioning Drew's frequent morning wanderings to his father. She had hoped that by reasoning with the boy she could convince him to postpone his exploratory hikes until after school. At once, Kate turned toward the door. She must report Drew's repeated tardiness to his father.

But she stopped. No. She couldn't report anything to McCall Adams. Kate was not prepared to face him again. Not now. Not after that moment when she had ached to feel his arms around her. Kate recalled her mother's recent telegram in which she almost demanded that Kate return to El Paso. But Kate had firmly stood by her decision to tutor Drew. Should she have listened to her mother? Kate could go home even today, if she chose.

With great dread, she contemplated Mr. Adams escorting her into Dogwood this very afternoon. With great dread, she wondered what would transpire. Yet, despite her dread, a flame of anticipation flickered. No, she would not assent to her mother's demands and return to El Paso. She would continue as Drew's tutor.

After some deliberation, Kate decided she would search for Drew herself. On the two previous occasions that he had "conveniently" disappeared before her arrival, she had seen him coming home from the same spot—an opening in the wood's thick thatch, across the pasture full of horses. With ample effort, which cost her a broken fingernail, Kate placed two large logs on the dying coals and hoped they would blaze before her return. She wrapped her black shawl closer around her chilled arms and opened the door. Setting her lips, Kate marched from the summer kitchen toward the pasture's wooden gate. Nervously, she eyed the numerous mares grazing with their half-grown offspring. Kate's experience with horses had been limited to sitting in an exquisite buggy while a well-groomed steed pulled her along. As she began timidly picking her way across the frigid, dew-laden pasture, Kate wished she had taken more pains in equestrian pursuits.

However, the gentle horses never pursued her, and Kate arrived at her destination in a matter of minutes. Hesitantly, she stepped from the open pasture and into another world. A world full of pines and maples and oaks. A world full of underbrush and the damp scent of decaying leaves. A world full of birds and squirrels and deer. The haven of nature.

"Drew!" Kate called as she picked her way across the path he had obviously taken, a path that looked like it had been in use for several years. "Drew!" she called again, determined to find the boy and demand that he postpone his walks until after studies.

Kate, continuing strict adherence to the pathway, walked for what felt like hours. At long last, she came upon a scene that stopped her in her tracks and left her startled beyond words.

four

McCall rushed into his sparse bedroom and closed the door. There was so much he needed to do this morning. A buyer was coming from Dallas this afternoon with the intent of purchasing stallions. McCall should be grooming the stallions instead of reliving his past, but he had left the chore to Bob Mosely, his hired hand, who really should be mending fences in the east pasture. Still, McCall's past beckoned him like a siren that he could not ignore. The log walls of his tiny room seemed to open their arms and draw him into another world where Melody still lived.

He stumbled across the braided rug toward the walnut dressing table in the corner—Melody's dressing table. McCall lowered himself onto the stool she had once used. He picked up her hairbrush by its whale-bone handle. A hairbrush which still held strands of his wife's silky dark hair. Tenderly, he stroked the tarnished silver picture frame that protected the aging photo of the woman who had stolen his heart. The daguerreotype's gray tones hid the mahogany hue of her soft hair, the sparkle of her pale blue eyes, the sun-kissed freshness of her skin.

Fourteen years. Had fourteen years actually lapsed since the horrible events that lead to her death? That fateful day seemed but hours removed. . . .

❧

McCall was long overdue to leave his father's bank in Dallas. He had been negotiating a loan for a prominent citizen who was opening yet another store, and the whole thing took hours longer than he anticipated. When he left, the sun was gradually descending in the western sky. Nightfall was imminent. McCall was supposed to have met Melody at Devenport's Fine Restaurant thirty minutes before he left. He hated to keep her waiting, so he decided against going home to his parent's mansion in order to change into one of his formal evening suits. His business suit would have to do. Melody would understand. She always understood. That was one of the things McCall liked most about her. She had the looks *and* disposition of an angel.

When McCall arrived at Devenport's, he expected to see Melody waiting in the receiving room. A quick scan of the ornate room, decorated in plush red velvet, Persian rugs, and brass mirrors, revealed no sign of Melody.

Supposing that Melody had already been seated, McCall approached the host, dressed in a black tuxedo. "Excuse me, Appleton," he said, nearing the tall, cherry table. "I am to meet Melody Graham. Has she been seated?"

"Ah. . .Mr. Adams! We were wondering if you and your lovely fiancée would be keeping your reservations." He produced a smile and eyed McCall over his wire-rimmed reading glasses. Many times, McCall had seen the host's long face take on a haughty air, especially if the guests weren't at the top of society. "Miss Graham has yet to arrive," Appleton continued. "Would you care to be seated until she arrives?"

"No, thank you. I'll wait in the receiving room." At first, McCall had been relieved that his sweet Melody had not been kept waiting. But once the relief assuaged, a new concern came over him. Where *was* Melody? She had never, absolutely *never*, been late for any of their appointments. As the top of the hour neared and guest after guest entered with no sign of Melody, McCall experienced a case of full-fledged panic.

Something was wrong. Dreadfully wrong. He knew it in the deepest recesses of his heart, now pounding with fear. McCall rushed from the restaurant and into his awaiting carriage. In no time, he maneuvered the horse onto Melody's street, lined with the ostentatious homes of the well-to-do. Within ten minutes of his hasty exit from the restaurant, McCall pounded on the door of the Graham's three-story, pillared home. The usually cheerful doorman, Jim Lowery, met McCall with the troubled look of tragedy.

McCall, strangely certain that some grave adversity had overtaken his beloved fiancée, grabbed Jim's arms. "Where is Melody? Do you know? Is she all right?"

Jim lowered his distraught eyes and floundered for any words. Seconds later, Melody's assigned maid, stricken and tearful, rushed down the massive, curved stairway. McCall released the doorman and rushed toward the tall, slender woman. Her wrinkled black face seemed set with grief. Now believing the worst, McCall swallowed against the nauseating bile rising in his throat.

"Melody. . .is she. . ." He grabbed Mrs. Thedford's trembling hands.

"She's in her room, Mistah Adams." A guarded sob.

McCall tackled the stairs two at a time. He had no idea which room was Melody's room, but he would find her. She must surely need him. Need him in a desperate manner.

"Oh. . .but you can't. . .you mustn't. . .she isn't in any kinda shape to be acceptin' callers. . . ."

He ignored the maid and continued opening and closing

the doors that lined the massive, ornate hallway. At long last, he came to a room from which uncontrolled sobbing echoed like bursts of agony, held long at bay. By this point, Mrs. Thedford, ever the timid lady, had reached him. She desperately grabbed at McCall's arm, begging him not to enter. "You mustn't see her now. She will never forgive me if'n I allow you to see her—"

McCall turned the brass doorknob and pushed against the door, which refused to budge.

"Her mother musta locked it," Mrs. Thedford sighed.

"Melody!" McCall yelled, now frantic to see his shattered fiancée. He relentlessly pounded the door. "Melody! It's McCall!"

Melody produced no answer, only renewed sobbing, more intense, more tragic.

Growing increasingly desperate, McCall gritted his teeth, turned the doorknob and slammed his shoulder against the door.

"No!" Mrs. Thedford wailed. "You mustn't! You can't! You're heapin' trouble on top of trouble. Can't you wait 'til tomorrow?"

McCall whirled to face the wrinkled maid. "She will see me now! I must see her. I must know what has happened to her. Why do you insist on keeping me in such suspense?" Perspiration now rolled down McCall's back, a product of his agitation and the heat of a summer night.

The doorknob rattled. A lock clicked. The door sighed as it swung inward, and Melody's mother, Lydia Graham, stood before him. Nothing but an older version of Melody, Mrs. Graham was known about town as an angel of light. Unlike many of the wealthy, who sought only to please themselves, Melody's mother made certain her inherited fortune fed the poor and clothed the needy. Even though McCall had seen her cry with the distress of the destitute, he had never seen her so broken as now. The genteel lady appeared to be mourning a death. Was Melody indeed dead? Were those sobs actually the wails of her mother?

McCall, now crazed, brushed past Mrs. Graham to see his beloved Melody, a crumpled, broken heap on her majestic, canopy bed. Her face buried in a pillow. Her body shaking with sobs. Her dress, torn and sullied. Oblivious to the codes of propriety, McCall rushed to Melody's side, sat on the edge of her bed, and pulled her into his arms. When she turned her face to his, McCall gasped at the sight of her swollen eyes and bleeding lips.

"Oh no. . ." McCall groaned, gathering Melody into his arms. "Oh no. . .no. . .no. . ." He held her tightly, and she clung to his lapel as a new onslaught of weeping wracked her thin body. "Have you sent for the doctor?" he demanded.

"Yes. Mr. Graham left only seconds before your arrival." Mrs. Graham choked back her own sob as she lowered herself to the end of Melody's bed. "I had just sent Mary down for some warm water."

As if on cue, Mary Thedford stopped hovering uncertainly near the doorway and dashed down the hallway.

"What happened?"

"I believe she. . .she. . .I cannot say it." Mrs. Graham covered her face while Melody clung to McCall as if he were her only link with sanity.

And McCall's worst suspicions were at last confirmed. Externally, he soothed Melody by gently stroking her hair and singing the love song he had written especially for her. Internally, McCall hurled every expletive he could conjure at the man who had done this to his beloved. Dashing all thoughts of biblical principles to the wind, McCall even plotted to kill the man if he found him.

The next few hours passed in a whirlwind of activity. After the doctor's examination and treatment, Melody was given a heavy sedative, which induced a sound sleep. While she slept, McCall requested an interview with Mr. Graham. The grim, stately gentleman ushered McCall into the shadowed library, which smelled of dried roses and musty books. Turning his back to McCall, Mr. Graham gazed out the floor-to-ceiling window, which opened onto the fragrant garden.

"I will understand if you feel that you must break the engagement with my daughter," Mr. Graham said, never taking his gaze from the garden, bathed in the full moon's light.

McCall choked on his own frustration and rushed to Mr. Graham's side. Didn't Melody's family understand just how desperately he loved her? "I was going to suggest just the opposite, Sir," McCall said respectfully. "Melody and I had planned to marry in the spring, but given the current circumstances, I–I wanted to suggest that perhaps the two of us should marry immediately."

Mr. Graham whirled to face McCall, his reddened eyes wide with astonishment. "Do you think your parents will support you in your decision once they know the truth?"

"They need not know."

"And how do you propose to keep it from them?"

"By requiring silence from everyone who knows of the situation. Who in your household knows?"

"Only the doorman and Melody's personal maid."

"Fine. We can tell them that if they tell a soul, they will

lose their job. Furthermore, by marrying Melody now, if. . . if by chance there is a child. . ."

"Then everyone will think it was simply a product of your marriage."

"Yes."

The gentleman, who only yesterday appeared youthful enough to be Melody's elder brother, now looked old enough to be her grandfather rather than her father. The effects of grief upon the carefree man's demeanor struck McCall. "And this in no way affects your love for her?" Mr. Graham asked.

"If this were to affect my love, it is indeed no love at all. . . ."

❧

McCall, still sitting at Melody's dressing table, wearily pressed his fingertips against his forehead. This time, there were no tears in reliving the memory, only a dull ache where there had once been an opened, gaping hole. He looked into the mirror and gazed into his own eyes. Eyes that only an hour ago had drunk in the beauty of Miss Kate Lowell—cheeks red with the cool autumn breeze, lips tilted in a pleasant smile. Those eyes seemed determined to betray Melody's memory. Some part of him demanded that he continue to cling to Melody while another part of him seemed resolved to think only of Kate. Her dark hair, her gentle spirit, her obvious devotion to God, her eyes—the color of hazelnuts. Something in McCall had urged him to take her in his arms, to feel her lips against his.

Deeply disgusted with himself, McCall fell to his knees beside the bed, gripping the homemade patchwork quilt in his clammy hands. In the last few years, with the help of

God's Spirit at work in his life, McCall moved from wanting to kill the man who assaulted his beloved Melody to recognizing his need to forgive. Although McCall still periodically struggled with bitterness, God seemed forever patient as He gently led McCall toward a forgiving heart. Furthermore, God had begun to heal the pain caused by McCall's family disavowing him when he chose to raise Drew. McCall often prayed that his heart would be filled with unconditional love for those who should have supported his decision. Part of the answer to that prayer manifested itself in the restoration of the relationship between McCall and his elder sister, Rebekah, who now resided on the East Coast. But during all his struggles to try to be the man God wanted him to be, McCall never imagined that God would be pleased if he forgot Melody.

"Oh Lord," he pleaded. "Please take these detestable desires from me. I know, beyond any doubt, that you sent Miss Lowell here in answer to my prayer for a tutor. Please, Lord, please, end this torture within my soul. Oh God, help me to look upon Kate Lowell as a sister, and nothing more. Surely, I could never truly love any other woman but Melody. That makes these feelings I'm having for Miss Lowell all the more abominable. . ."

But in the midst of McCall's heavenward cry came a strong thought that left him distraught: *Release the past.* McCall blinked in stunned disbelief. How could McCall ever relinquish all that had happened? He couldn't. He wouldn't. No. This thought was not of God. It could never be of God. But he recalled his prior musings about God's intent in placing Miss Lowell at the ranch. Could the Lord actually be encouraging a romance that involved a man who was in no way ready for romance? The thought left

McCall dismayed. Standing, he stiffly walked toward his bedroom door. He would not entertain these thoughts any further. McCall simply was not ready for another woman in his life, and God knew that.

But what if it were God's will for you to fall in love with Miss Lowell? Would you be willing to follow such a plan for your life?

The disturbing question stopped McCall as if he had slammed into a wall. With his mind still reeling from this emotional blow, McCall dashed from his log home and back toward his horse-grooming chores in the barn. McCall could, in no way, fathom that God would ask him to relinquish his feelings for Melody. He might as well put to death a part of his soul.

five

Not believing her eyes, Kate blinked against the bright streaks of sunlight filtering through the thick trees. She had followed the path in the woods to a river that rushed along a wide, sandy bed. The smell of cold, fresh water wafted toward her senses as she examined the massive fallen tree trunk that spanned from one bank to the other. On that fallen tree tottered Drew, his arms extended for balance, as he followed another boy, dressed in faded overalls, who likewise walked across the fallen tree. Kate had seen this boy only once before—a boy with white-blond hair, a pug nose, and a stubborn set to his lips. Kate was certain this was none other than Calvin Wilcox, the boy with whom Drew had fought the day Kate agreed to the tutoring position.

As Kate studied them from her unobserved post, the two boys laughed companionably, as if they had been friends their whole lives. Deliberating her options, Kate chewed her lower lip. Should she reveal herself and demand Drew's return to the schoolroom? Or should she simply go back to the room and wait for him to return on his own? Should Kate report this incident to Mr. Adams? She couldn't imagine that he would want his son playing with Calvin, not after Wilcox had so blatantly disclosed his hostile intent. Furthermore, why wasn't Calvin in school himself?

"Calvin! Calvin Wilcox! Where are you, boy?" a bear-like voice growled from the other side of the river.

Kate impulsively stepped behind a massive oak. Her heart pounding in dread, she peered around the tree to see both boys scramble from the fallen log. Calvin urgently pointed toward a hollow spot along the river's tall bank, much like a shallow cave. Drew skidded down the sandy bank on his backside and scrambled toward the concave hiding place.

"Calvin! Where are you?" Wilcox demanded once more.

"Right here, Pa," Calvin bellowed, his nonchalant walk matching his carefree voice. Kate marveled that only seconds before Calvin had urgently instructed Drew to hide. He casually bent to pick up a cane pole, a wooden bucket, and a basket full of fish. "I've been fishing," he said as his father appeared from amongst the thick thatch of trees on the opposite bank.

"Fishing?" The angular Wilcox, who carried a rifle, looked down at his son in such a critical, scornful manner that Kate pitied young Calvin. Next, Eugene scanned the river as if he were looking for someone. "Did I hear you talkin' to someone?" he barked.

"See! Ma can cook 'em for dinner." Calvin proudly held up the basket full of fish as if he were trying to divert his father's attention. "I found a school of minnows and dipped 'em out of the river then used 'em for bait." He sloshed the bucket of water for emphasis.

"I kept ya home from school today to help me in the fields, not fish!" Eugene greedily grabbed the basket of fish. "Now go dig those sweet 'taters like I told you to."

"But Pa, Ma said we didn't have no meat for dinner today. I thought you'd be glad I caught so many—"

Eugene slapped Calvin on the side of his head and shoved him forward. "Just shut up and get to work."

Kate's stomach twisted in pity for Calvin. The Wilcoxes obviously needed the fish for their dinner. Why couldn't Eugene praise his son's efforts instead of treating him so harshly?

As Calvin picked his way through the underbrush, Eugene turned and examined the river again. "I coulda sworn I heard you talkin' to someone," he growled as he fell in behind his son.

Calvin maintained his silence and a startled buck instantly distracted Eugene. He dropped the fish basket, aimed, and fired his weapon.

Kate jumped as her ears rang with the gun's explosion.

A long stream of expletives followed as Wilcox watched the deer bound into the woods' thick underbrush. Eugene pulled a bottle of whisky from his pocket and took a long swallow, then he picked up the basket full of fish and silently followed his son. Kate released her pent-up breath as she realized the deer had so distracted Eugene that he forgot to further question Calvin about the person to whom he had been talking.

She watched until the father and son were nowhere to be seen or heard. At last, Drew scrambled up the river's bank, sand and fallen leaves softly crunching under his boots. Kate stepped from behind her hasty hiding spot. Her arms folded, she silently watched her pupil cautiously pick his way back over the fallen tree trunk that spanned the river. Tongue between his teeth, he hopped onto her side of the bank. Drew bent to brush the damp sand from his fresh denims before starting toward the path on which she stood. Drew casually glanced up to see Kate and stopped, his eyes round in shock.

"Miss Lowell! What are you—"

"I came to find you, Drew Adams! What do you think you're doing, wandering off in the woods when it's time for school?" Kate said in her firmest voice. She had never found it necessary to discipline a tardy boy before. The authoritative tone of her own voice amazed her.

"Ah, Miss Lowell. . ." Drew, hanging his head, kicked at a protruding root with the tip of his boot. "I get so bored sitting in that room all day long, I just—"

"And what in the world has transpired between you and Calvin Wilcox?" Kate interrupted.

"We're friends now!" Drew said, his dark eyes bright with expectation.

"How did that happen? Two weeks ago, if I remember correctly, the two of you weren't on the friendliest terms."

"Oh that, Calvin just needed somebody to call his bluff, that's all. Once I showed him he couldn't bully me, he came around."

Kate often curiously mused that Drew didn't resemble his father, but she couldn't deny that he possessed McCall's mannerisms and turns of phrase. "I'm assuming the Wilcox's land must meet yours along here somewhere?"

"Yes Ma'am," Drew said, moving past Kate to walk along the path.

Kate fell into step behind him.

"Calvin says they just bought the land from Mr. Parker. They used to farm the land for him. Now they own it."

"Well," Kate continued, glancing up at the back of Drew's head, "do you think it's wise to develop such a friendship with Calvin, considering his father's recent outburst?"

"I'm not afraid of his father," Drew said bravely. A dove's gentle cooing filtered through the expanse of trees and wrapped its sound around them.

"Does your father know of your friendship with Calvin?"

"No ma'am." Drew spun to face her. "And please don't tell him. Dad never lets me have friends. I get so tired of—of being all alone. Calvin is the only friend I have right now."

Drew's dark, pleading eyes touched the very bottom of Kate's heart. She had silently observed Mr. Adams' protective tendencies toward Drew. Considering Drew's mixed heritage and the reactions of folks like the tutor at the train station, Kate couldn't say that she blamed Mr. Adams very much. Nonetheless, the impact of such shielding must be tremendously stifling to a free-spirited fourteen-year-old boy.

"Please promise you won't tell Dad," Drew pressed again.

Kate swallowed against a throat as dry as the autumn leaves, falling one by one from the surrounding trees. At once, she felt torn between allegiance to the boy she had grown extremely fond of and his handsome father who employed her. At long last, a thought struck her, and she spoke. "I won't tell your father if—"

"Oh, thank you, Miss Lowell!" The exuberant Drew grabbed her hands.

"I won't tell your father *if* you promise not to come to the woods any more until *after* lessons, and *if* you promise to use the utmost discretion in your friendship. I do not believe it would be wise for Wilcox to discover that Calvin and you are friends."

"I promise! I promise! I'll just tell Calvin to meet me in the afternoons. That'll work out better anyway since he has to go to school most mornings. And we wouldn't dare tell his father. . .or mine." A thoughtful glimmer danced through Drew's eyes. "I wish Dad would let me go to school with Calvin," he muttered.

A stab of disappointment entered Kate's chest. Was Drew not happy with her as a teacher?

As if Drew could read Kate's mind, he interjected, "Oh. . . not that I don't like you Miss Lowell. I–I–It's just that I would so like to know what other boys my age are up to." His voice squeaked on the final words, attesting to his emerging manhood.

"I understand," Kate said, squeezing Drew's arm. And the truth was, Kate understood too well. So well that she ached for the boy who seemed to have no idea that his mixed heritage would stalk him for life.

As they walked back through the dense trees and toward the pasture, full of horses, a new thought struck Kate. A new thought that spawned raging curiosity. What was Drew's mother like? She must have been a beautiful, gracious woman to have stolen McCall Adams' heart. Kate pondered how McCall had come to know and fall in love with an Indian woman. His wife must have been full of charm and wisdom. Absently, she wondered if Mr. Adams possessed any photos. Perhaps there were some in the log cabin.

Immediately, Kate put an end to such thoughts. Mr. Adams had never once invited her into his log cabin. She and Drew usually shared their noon meal in the summer kitchen or they picnicked under a tree. If she did find a valid reason to be in McCall's home, Kate would not become a snoop in order to satisfy her inquisitive interests. As she followed Drew through the pasture's gate and toward the schoolroom, Kate couldn't deny her deep curiosity concerning the kind of woman whom McCall

Adams would love. If he were ever to invite Kate into his home, she would certainly not decline the opportunity to view any photos that were in clear view.

Amazingly, the opportunity to see a photo of McCall's wife presented itself, with no effort from Kate, within a matter of weeks.

&

By early December, Kate realized Mr. Adams' determination, at all costs, to avoid her. While Drew silently calculated his math equations, Kate watched out the window as Mr. Adams masterfully broke in a gray dappled stallion. After that one morning when McCall had escorted her from the hotel to the ranch, he had arranged for his hired hand, Bob Mosely, to drive Kate. From that day until now, Kate only caught momentary glimpses of her employer. Despite herself, she began to greedily consume those glimpses. His square jaw line. The aristocratic nose. His close-set dark eyes and heavy brows. The lean form of his powerful frame.

Today, Mr. Adams wore his usual pullover denim shirt and worn leather jacket, dark riding pants, the ever-present black hat, and frayed working gloves. As the stallion repeatedly lowered his head, kicked his feet, and stirred clouds of dust into the cold, morning air, McCall rode in rhythm, seeming to second-guess the angry horse's every move. The stocky Mr. Mosely stood on the wooden fence that encompassed the corral, whooping as if McCall were a hero of war. At long last, the stallion calmed, snorting as he ran the circumference of the corral until he stopped and haughtily raised his head, ears pricked. McCall stroked the horse's pale gray neck; his concentration focused solely on the task at hand.

Then, as if he felt her watching him, Mr. Adams glanced

toward the summer kitchen and directly into the window where Kate stood. Her stomach felt like it dropped to her feet as she was once more entranced by McCall Adams' warm appraisal. They might as well have been in the carriage all over again, reliving that moment when he placed his coat around her. The coat he wore now. Kate's arms warmed as if he had indeed placed it around her shoulders, and she could almost smell the odor of leather mixed with horses once more.

Their gaze continued, and the emotions Kate had suppressed for weeks would no longer be stifled. She felt as if the man might as well have kissed her. There was no denying the attraction Mr. Adams held for her. Even at this distance, his expression burned with open admiration. Kate, certain she was just as transparent, could do little to hide her feelings. Kate's mother had painstakingly taught her the art of maintaining a cool demeanor, during any circumstance. But since the moment she met Mr. Adams and Drew, Kate had somehow stepped out of that upper society style of conduct

She should go home to El Paso. Now. Before this. . .this senseless hopelessness between her and Mr. Adams escalated into something neither of them wanted. Kate was not prepared to ever lose her heart again as she had with Zachary. His death had almost devastated her. Kate remembered, day after day, returning to his grave and sobbing until she collapsed. She remembered her irrational anger at Travis Campbell, who took Zach's accidental death as hard as Kate did. She didn't know if she could mentally survive another deep loss. There were times in the midst of her grief that she wondered if she were, indeed, going insane.

Kate had nothing against the possibilities of marriage. A marriage of convenience would suit her nicely. Nonetheless, she could not and would not ever give her heart to another man the way she had given it to Zachary. The prospect left her shaking in dread of what new pain that might involve.

As her legs trembled and she continued to be held captive by McCall's steady appraisal, Kate recognized, once and for all, that this man presented a dire threat to her need to forevermore withhold her heart. Not that she had, by any means, fallen in love with him. But Kate could no longer deny that too much time with McCall Adams would prove emotionally fatal.

The flames that crackled in the fireplace might as well have been the sounds of Kate's own emotions, stirred by the fire pulsing within her veins. McCall Adams was exactly the kind of man who arrested Kate. A man of strength and dignity. A man of strong faith. A man who would never turn his back on one in need. Over the last weeks, she had seen McCall give meals and a strong horse to two different, weary families, down on their luck, crossing the country on foot, in search of work and a place to call home. McCall was a stark contrast to the refined men in El Paso who wore their Christianity like a fine suit. McCall Adams lived his faith. He was genuine. And Kate was, without question, mesmerized.

A light tap on her shoulder stirred Kate from her reverie, and she spun to face Drew, his dancing, dark eyes full of questions. "What has you so distracted, Miss Lowell? I've asked you the same question three times." Drew glanced out the window in the very direction where Kate had been looking.

"Oh, I'm so sorry, I just. . ." As she trailed off helplessly, her cheeks grew exceptionally warm and she nervously stepped toward Drew's desk.

The boy watched her, a speculative gleam in his eyes, and Kate knew, with a sense of dread, that Drew understood more than she ever wished.

"What was your question?" she asked, leaning over the page full of math equations that Drew had meticulously solved.

"I was just asking you to check over my work and wondering if I might go for a walk now. I thought I'd see if I could add to our leaf collection." He moved toward the fragrant fire, grabbed a poker, and jabbed at the flaming logs.

As she had suspected in recent weeks, Kate realized with certainty that Drew had grown at least an inch since her arrival two months ago. His ever-present denims, now much too short, attested to his growth spurt.

And Drew's keen eye for detail attested to his brilliance. While Kate had joyously embraced the opportunity to tutor such an intelligent lad, she now wished he weren't quite so astute in his powers of observation. Kate forced herself to examine the math problems, finding only one small error.

"You may go, if you like," she said, wanting more than anything, to be left alone. Alone for prayer. Kate desperately needed to seek God's guidance concerning the possibility of her leaving Dogwood. . .soon. Out of the corner of her eye, she saw Drew hesitating and she cringed with the tension that had sprung between them.

"Dad likes you," Drew said at last.

Kate looked up. "What?" she gasped in reply.

"Dad likes you," Drew repeated in a very practical tone. She produced a shaky, polite smile, while her heart whispered confirmation of Drew's admission. "Whatever would make you say something like that, Drew Adams?" Kate said in a fondly scolding tone.

Drew shrugged. "Just because I catch him watching you off and on, especially in the morning when Mr. Mosely arrives with you. It's like he waits at the kitchen window while I finish my breakfast until he sees you arrive. Yesterday morning, he even called me 'Kate' instead of 'Drew.' " The boy produced a dry cough.

Nonplussed, Kate glanced toward the dark, wooden floor and made a monumental job of examining the shadows from the flickering fire as they danced hither and yon.

"And I can't say that I blame him. . .for–for watching you," Drew continued in a halting voice.

Kate once more was compelled to look into Drew's eyes, now churning with emotion.

"Miss Lowell. . .you're so beautiful," he announced awkwardly, his face flushing.

She swallowed against the lump in her throat that threatened to choke her as she recognized a full-blown case of puppy love. "I–I don't know what to say, Drew. Of course, I'm–I'm flattered by your–your admiration, but–but. . ."

"Oh, I know I'm much too young for you," he continued helplessly. "But Dad isn't."

Truly stunned, she blinked and began a desperate, silent plea for heavenly deliverance from this awkward moment.

"I don't think he's even looked at another woman since mother—except you."

"Do you remember your mother, Drew?" Kate asked, relieved to grab onto a subject that would deliver her from the present line of conversation.

"No, of course not. She died when I was born."

"Oh."

"All I have are a few photos of her."

"Oh?" Kate's ongoing curiosity about McCall's wife resurrected itself in oversized proportions.

"Yes. Would you like to see her photo? I keep it in my desk."

"Well, I. . ."

With no encouragement from Kate, Drew walked toward the pine table, which served as his desk. He pulled open the bottom side drawer and extracted a picture frame that looked to be fine pewter, much like the ones her mother purchased from the silversmith.

"There she is. She was beautiful, wasn't she? Dad says I take after her."

Kate, trembling with expectation, took the extended photo and looked into the face of a woman who held no traces of Indian heritage. Kate's mind whirled with questions as she glanced from the photo to Drew and back to the photo. There was a marked resemblance between Drew and the woman, who possessed a sweet, candid tilt to her fine-boned face. She and Drew shared the same forehead and generous mouth. But Drew's obvious Indian traits varied greatly from any other facial features that his mother possessed, or that McCall possessed, for that matter.

"Yes. . .yes, I think you do take after her," Kate said gently, astounded at the implications of this photo. She continued to silently stare at the picture's varying shades of gray until they blurred. Vaguely, she acknowledged Drew's repeated request for a walk in the woods and gave him permission to leave.

When the door opened minutes later, Kate glanced up from her perusal of the photo, expecting to see Drew. Instead, she encountered the questioning eyes of McCall Adams. The pewter frame seemed to burn in Kate's hand, and her face warmed far past comfort.

"I noticed Drew going toward the woods. Did you give. . . him. . .permission. . .to. . ." McCall's words trailed to a stop as he glanced toward Kate's hands.

She resisted the urge to hide the picture behind her back.

six

Despite his personal pledge to avoid Kate, McCall continued to look for an excuse—any excuse—to approach her.
The last several weeks of watching Kate without speaking
to her had been something close to torment. When he saw
Drew traipsing off to the woods, McCall knew he had
found his excuse to speak with the lovely tutor.

But seeing her holding Melody's photo left McCall's
insides churning in rage. He felt as though Kate had
somehow violated his privacy and his memory of the wife
he still loved. "How *dare* you snoop in Drew's desk!"
McCall accused. Closing the distance between them, he
jerked the photo from her hands.

"I didn't snoop! I didn't even ask to see the photo.
Drew retrieved it and asked me to look at it. How dare
you accuse *me* of snooping!"

"You could have declined the offer!" McCall demanded,
his face only inches from Kate's.

"He gave me little choice!" she said in a voice just as
challenging as his. "Drew pulled the picture from his desk
and placed it in my hands before I had the chance to
decline."

· McCall fully expected Miss Lowell to back down from
him. Yet her flashing hazel eyes, flared nostrils, and firm
lips showed no signs that her retreat was even a remote
possibility. Her strong will both shocked and perplexed
McCall. He never anticipated this much determination

from such an exquisite lady.

Thoughts of apologizing flitted through McCall's jumbled mind. But those considerations had precious little opportunity to mature into words as other disturbing reflections muddled his mind. Reflections of Kate's flushed cheeks and the soft contour of her narrow nose. Reflections of the golden spokes that darted from her pupils to add a hint of intrigue to her eyes. Reflections of how her dark hair, glistening in the dim firelight, would feel under his touch. Reflections of the weeks and weeks and weeks he had silently watched her disembark Bob Mosely's wagon. Reflections of the moment that left him as weak as a newborn colt when he caught her watching him from the window.

McCall hadn't held a woman in fourteen years—not since he clutched Melody and watched her slip into a coma. But standing here in this schoolroom, McCall couldn't even remember why he was angry. All he could think was how much he wanted to feel Miss Kate Lowell's lips kissing his.

The room seemed to shimmer with the force of McCall's emotions. Kate's determined expression softened to one of mystique and attraction. McCall, reacting from the moment, did what he had wanted to do when he caught Kate watching him. He stroked her cheek with the back of his fingers. Her quick breath, her bottom lip caught between her teeth only added to McCall's own reactions. Kate's skin was as soft as he had ever imagined. The sweet scent of her rose perfume propelled him to move all the closer and brush his lips ever so gently against hers.

McCall half expected Miss Lowell to pull away. When she didn't, he reached for her arms with the intent of lengthening the kiss. But McCall, mesmerized by the moment, forgot about the treasured photo he held. When he clasped Kate's arms, the frame fell from his hand and crashed against the floor.

The jarring sound of shattering glass seemed to awaken McCall's common sense. *Melody. . .Melody. . .Melody.* He had forgotten all about her. And, in the forgetting, he had destroyed the glass that protected her precious photo. McCall abruptly stepped away from Kate, now disgusted with his jagged breathing, with his thoughtless reaction to this exquisite lady.

She immediately stooped to pick up the shards of broken glass. "I'm so sorry," Kate muttered, as though she had been the one who broke it.

"It wasn't your fault," McCall heard himself say, feeling as if he were still trapped under the spell of Kate's beauty. He bent to assist her, only to have their hands descend upon the frame in exactly the same spot. Kate's pliable, warm hand stilled under his and trembled against his callused palm. Once more, the room seemed to fill with his raging emotions. McCall's stomach churned with the warm response he had worked so hard to deny since the first time he set eyes on Kate. As hard as he had prayed, as much as he wanted to remain loyal to Melody, as disgusted as he was with himself, McCall still found Miss Lowell fascinating.

Realizing the horrid irony of his present situation, McCall observed their hands, touching over Melody's photo. The sight gave him the strength to release Kate's hand, grab the pewter frame, and stalk toward the door.

"You're still in love with her, aren't you?" Kate whispered. Her voice sounded like the faint rustling of dry leaves stirred by a chilling winter breeze.

McCall, angered by her observation, whirled to face the woman who only seconds before he had kissed. Her crest-fallen demeanor did little to calm his churning stomach and raging soul. "That's none of your business," he snapped, his voice sounding tormented, even to his own ears. "I didn't hire you to question my feelings."

"And did you hire me with plans to kiss me?" she demanded, her fists clenched at her side.

"I hired you to tutor my son. Period!"

"Is he *really* your son?" Kate blurted. Immediately she covered her mouth with the tips of her shaking fingers as if she were as shocked by own her words as McCall.

"How dare you." McCall growled, his paternal protection making him despise the idea of Kate's understanding the truth that no one in Dogwood but Dr. Engle knew. "That is none of your business."

"And what about Drew? Is it *his* business?" She rushed to a straight-backed chair near the fireplace and gripped the top rail until her knuckles were white.

"Drew—"

"How much longer do you think you can keep the truth from him? Do you honestly think the boy will continue on, blissfully thinking he just takes after his mother?"

McCall's face chilled. While he knew he couldn't indefinitely hide the truth from Drew, McCall had hoped to postpone that inevitable day of reckoning for a few more years.

"Were you ever even married to her?" Kate continued, as if the question were wrenched from her.

New fury churned through McCall's veins. His forehead beaded in sweat. "How can you suggest. . . You never even knew her!" He took several deliberate steps toward Kate and lowered his face to within inches of hers once more. Her responding flinch was barely discernible. "I will tell you one time, and one time only, and you'd better listen closely," he said in a menacing, measured tone. "Melody was forced into something she never wanted; I arrived at her house and found her beaten and sobbing in her mother's arms. She never even got a good look at the man's face—we didn't even know he was an Indian until Drew was born. She was my fiancée at the time. I could have very easily broken our engagement and no one—*no one* would have blamed me. I married her two days later because I *loved* her." A knot formed in McCall's throat. "And given the slight chance that there was to be a child, I wanted to do everything in my power to protect Melody's dignity."

Kate's eyes widened in dismay as the full force of the truth struck her. "I'm–I'm t–terribly. . .t–terribly sorry," she stammered, her own face growing pale. "I should have never. . .I have been dreadfully—" With the swish of her forest green skirt, Kate turned from him and approached the rock fireplace. She crossed her arms and kept her back to him, her shoulders hunched.

McCall, gritting his teeth, whipped open the door and stalked onto the yard. With a rush, the cool afternoon air met the perspiration on his neck and forehead and produced an icy shiver down his spine. McCall paused, observing the winter sun proudly projecting its bright afternoon rays across the expanse of his property. The sun bathed McCall's world in golden light. The corral. The pasture full of horses. The massive barn. His small log cabin. But the sun had not shone on his heart for fourteen years. Not really. Oh, Drew had brought him an enormous amount of joy, and McCall had done everything in his power to be a good father. . .for Melody's sake. . .for his own sake. But deep inside, McCall was as cold as ice.

Release the past.

Just as that thought had intruded his mind and disturbed his quiet times over the last few weeks, it once more seemed to come from nowhere. McCall wanted to rend his hair with the anguish this thought delivered. How could he ever release his hold on the past? How could he ever release his love for Melody?

He rushed across the expanse of the yard that separated his home from the summer kitchen. Taking huge, determined strides, he stepped up onto his rough-hewn porch. McCall whipped open the door, slammed it behind him, and crashed onto the horsehair sofa. He tossed the shattered frame onto the sofa and threw his hat across the room. In despair over his wretched situation, McCall placed his elbows on his knees, and grabbed his head in his hands. He curled his callused fingers into his hair until it felt as if he were pulling the hair out by the roots.

Melody. . .Melody. . .Melody.

He tried with all his might to conjure her image, but all McCall saw was the wide-eyed beauty he had just kissed. With a groan, he leaned back, closed his eyes, and desperately tried to pray. But no words would come.

As if his heart were bent on tormenting him, he at long last *did* recall Melody's image. Melody, shortly after Drew's birth, clutching at McCall's shirt as if she were clutching at life. After the forty-hour labor, the doctor had sadly shaken his head and said she had begun to hemorrhage and had lost entirely too much blood. McCall, choking on his own sobs had begged Melody to stay with him. Up until the baby was born, McCall had respected the delicacy of her emotional and physical condition, never touching her in the way a husband knew a wife. But he had hoped, desperately hoped, that perhaps Melody's broken heart would mend and they would be able to begin a true marriage after she recovered from giving birth. Now he watched all his hopes, all his dreams. . .his Melody weakly clinging to her last breaths.

Just before she went into the coma, she gripped McCall's shirt and said, "Promise me you'll. . .you'll keep little. . . little Drew. P—Promise me. I. . .I cannot explain it to you, b—but I love. . .love him. H—He is a part of. . .of me. . . even. . .even though. . .I would have never. . .never wished it. . .so. . ."

"I promise. I promise. I promise," McCall had repeated like a mad man. He desperately wanted to deny the significance of Melody's request. He wanted to beg her to fight for her life. Instead, McCall had promised and then watched her slip away, into a coma, and from the coma into the arms of death.

During those following days, McCall was so numb from pain, so consumed with the funeral and the family gathering, so caught-up in the task of finding a wet nurse, that he was blind to the intents of his immediate family. Melody's family was honored that he would even consider raising Drew. They offered both financial and moral support. McCall's family reacted in the opposite manner. Once they actually saw baby Drew, McCall's parents demanded the truth of his conception. Shortly thereafter, Mr. and Mrs. Adams arranged a private, surprise meeting with McCall and a woman who ran an orphanage. She grudgingly said she would take the baby off his hands for a substantial fee. When McCall refused, his parents were aghast that their son would risk the family reputation for a child who wasn't even his.

McCall relived that moment with vivid clarity. He stood in the ornate library at his parent's mansion, glaring at both of his elite parents and that plump, greedy redhead who wanted to take little Drew away.

"I promised Melody I would raise Drew myself, and I *will* raise him," McCall growled. "He might not be mine. But he is Melody's. I loved her. And I *will* love him." Out of the corner of his eye, he saw the library door inch open and his grandfather's wrinkled face appear in the opening. The sight of that face of character only increased McCall's determination. Pa Adams, who had been like a father to McCall, had been the only one in the Adams household who, from the onset, knew the whole truth of Melody's tragic circumstances. The kindly retired doctor had been nothing but a source of strength through the whole ordeal.

As the tense silence continued, the mantel clock ticked off the seconds, sounding more like a death toll than a timepiece.

At long last, his father spoke, slowly and deliberately. "If you do not release this. . .this. . .illegitimate. . .we will be forced to ask you to leave. For good."

McCall, rigid with rage, had stomped from the room to be greeted by his pale grandfather. "I will help you," Pa Adams said, gripping McCall's arms. And he did. Within the week, the dear, sickly saint had signed over every penny he owned to McCall and Drew, and the three of them moved into quarters of their own. A year later, Pa Adams went to meet the Lord, and Drew started his horse ranch in Dogwood.

The whole horrid story, fourteen years removed, still seemed as fresh in McCall's mind as if it had happened yesterday. He kept these events locked tightly within his heart's cold corridor, where the sun never shone. In that icy chamber, the story remained preserved and fresh; the pain, although dulled with the years, still lived to be recalled at any given moment.

Release the past.

"How? How? How?" he roared heavenward. McCall stood. With a vengeance, he retrieved his hat from across the room, crammed it back onto his head, and left the cabin, deliberately walking toward the spot in the woods where he had seen Drew disappear.

McCall would focus on the practical necessities of the moment and once more ignore that disturbing thought that suggested he put the past behind him. And the practical necessities of *this* moment involved finding out why his son was wandering through the woods when he should be studying.

seven

Kate scurried from one corner of the summer kitchen to the other, retrieving the few pencils and books that belonged to her. Once she arranged her possessions in a neat pile, she began straightening Drew's papers and books. At last, she grabbed the straw broom from its spot in the corner and swept up the last shards of broken glass.

She was leaving. She was leaving and not coming back. Kate would go home, back to El Paso. Never, absolutely never, would she return to Dogwood. For any reason.

After Mr. Adams' recent behavior and obvious love for his deceased wife, Kate fully realized the futility—yes, the blind stupidity—of continuing on as Drew's tutor. The situation was beyond volatile. Furthermore, Kate was well on the road to completely and irrevocably losing her heart to this tall, lean man, with his captivating eyes and hidden heart. And that was one loss she simply could not risk.

"Now!" she said aloud, gazing around the room to see if she'd left anything out of place. Satisfied with the neat appearance, Kate grabbed her reticule and light shawl, both hanging from a peg near the door. She wrapped the shawl around her arms, picked up her books and pencils, and reached for the doorknob.

As the cold metal contacted her already chilled palm, an equally chilling thought left her spine tingling. *You have not once stopped to pray about your hasty decision. What if it is God's will for you to stay? What if it is God's will for you to give your heart to Mr. Adams?*

Kate gripped the doorknob. She stared into the smoldering fire. She pressed her trembling lips together. At once, Kate felt as if she were involved in a battle of wills. Some still, small voice in the bottom of her soul whispered for her to stay, but her mind demanded she behave rationally and leave immediately. She should go this instant, find Mr. Mosely, and ask him to take her back to the hotel.

Her contemplative gaze fell upon Drew's desk and his pile of graded papers. Kate's heart twisted with thoughts of leaving the boy. Every day her fondness for Drew had grown. She was one of a precious few connections he had to the outside world. He would be so disappointed if Kate left.

She should at least leave him a note, explaining that her decision was in no way a product of her feelings for him. Kate, rushing to his desk, plopped down her books and reticule. The top book, Kate's Bible, toppled over and plunked open to release a dried red rose. The last rose Zachary gave Kate before his death. She slowly picked up the fading flower and held it to her nose, inhaling the faint, sweet odor. With the rose, Zachary had bestowed a gentle kiss upon Kate's waiting lips. Immediately, she compared that kiss to the one Mr. Adams and she had shared. Her face heated with the drastic difference in her response to Mr. Adams and her response to Zachary. Regardless of her love for him, Zachary had never stirred her as Mr. Adams had stirred her. This realization only heightened Kate's determination to leave. She placed the dried rose back into the Bible and firmly shut its pages.

Trembling anew, she grabbed a sheet of the coarse paper she found in the top drawer. Kate positioned her pencil over the empty page, bit her lips, and debated about how to begin. But she could never get past "Dear Drew." After several frustrating seconds of racking her brain, Kate's eyes began to sting. What a horrid predicament to be in, feeling as if she must flee the father, yet knowing her fleeing would betray the son in the deepest sense.

The determined pounding of boots against firm ground diverted her attention. The footsteps neared the kitchen's doorway and stopped only long enough for the door to fling open. McCall, his face dark with anger, stepped into the room, followed by Drew, his head lowered, his eyes downcast.

McCall opened his mouth to speak, only to hesitate and briefly glance at the shawl Kate wore and her posture. A momentary expression of understanding flashed across his face before he narrowed his eyes and spoke.

"I just found Drew playing with Calvin Wilcox. Drew tells me you gave him permission to befriend Calvin," he growled as if Kate were guilty of the most heinous of crimes.

Kate looked from the downtrodden Drew, to his father, and back to Drew. "Yes. I did," she said defensively.

"How dare you go behind my back and allow a friendship you knew full well I would never approve!"

She deposited her pencil on the desk and turned to fully face McCall. "The child needs a friend," she said evenly. "I'm not going to tell you I wasn't concerned about Mr. Wilcox's attitude, but I admonished Drew to use discretion. How long do you think you are going to be able to keep him under lock and key, Mr. Adams? He is starved for friendship!"

"That is none of your business!" McCall walked across the room until he was once more standing within inches of Kate. "And furthermore, you have no right to approve such things. You should have referred him to me."

"Why? So you could tell him 'no' and keep him isolated his whole life?"

"I'm trying to protect him."

"Or trying to control him!"

"He's my son. I *should* control him."

"No! You should *lead* him. There's a *huge* difference!"

"For a woman who has no children, you are amazingly astute on the subject, Miss Lowell," he said sarcastically.

"I know enough to know you are gripping Drew so tightly the poor boy can hardly breathe!" she yelled in frustration. "And you're becoming a slave to your own control."

"What's that supposed to mean?"

"It's supposed to mean that it's an all-consuming job to hang onto someone to the degree you're hanging onto Drew. You don't have time for a life of your own because you're spending every spare moment making certain Drew is protected."

"Listen woman." He grabbed her upper arms, his eyes the glittering orbs of an angered panther.

"No, you listen, *Mr. Adams*." Gritting her teeth, Kate jerked away from his grip. "You might be able to intimidate every other woman you've ever known, but you *will not* intimidate me. So you might as well stop trying." Kate, her stomach churning, her legs about to collapse, could not believe the firmness, the self-assurance with which she uttered those words. She felt far from the bravado she claimed. But Kate would never let McCall Adams know that.

"Furthermore," she continued, narrowing her eyes once more. "I admonished Drew from the onset to take extra precaution in his dealings with Calvin. He understood that if Mr. Wilcox found out—"

"Let's not discuss Wilcox right now, especially not in front of. . ." Pressing his lips together, McCall trailed off as if he were frustrated with his own words.

"Why not, Dad?" Drew asked. "Do you think I don't know why Mr. Wilcox doesn't like me?"

Kate, stunned by what Drew might say, joined McCall in silently studying him.

"I know he calls me a 'stinkin' Injun.' And I also know that's because I am–am part Indian." Drew studied the tips of his boots.

"How do you know that?" McCall asked, his face ashen.

"A few months ago, I asked Dr. Engle some–some questions." Drew's intense dark eyes now scrutinized his father.

"And?"

"And he told me that. . .that you–you adopted me."

Silently, McCall rubbed a tired hand over his weary face. "And what else did he tell you, Drew?"

"That was all. That's all I know. But. . .but. . .he shuffled his feet uncomfortably. I'd certainly like to know the whole story. . .sometime."

"Why didn't you ask me in the first place?"

The boy shrugged his shoulders and helplessly looked toward Kate.

"Perhaps he simply wasn't. . .wasn't comfortable with that prospect," she supplied with an encouraging note.

McCall produced a weary sigh, stuffed his hands in his pockets, and walked toward the fireplace. He placed his arm along the rugged mantel and rested his forehead against his arm.

"May I. . .may I go now?" Drew asked.

"Yes. That's fine. Go do your chores," McCall said in a tight voice.

Drew silently left the summer kitchen and closed the door behind him.

Kate braced herself for another outburst from her angry employer but determined to remain calm.

"You were leaving and not coming back." He turned to face her. "Am I correct?" His measured words surprised Kate more than any amount of yelling would have.

"You are correct."

"Why?"

She suppressed a sarcastic snort. "Why do you think, Mr. Adams?"

Lips tightly together, he silently appraised Kate until she felt more than uncomfortable. Nevertheless, she refused to flinch from his scrutiny.

"Would it make any difference if I apologized?" he said at last.

Kate blinked. Once more, the man had completely taken her by surprise. "For what do you contemplate apologizing?"

He walked toward the window and silently stared toward the rolling, east Texas hills, full of barren trees and evergreens. "I think you know full well," he said at last.

"You mean for everything?"

"Yes, everything."

So much had happened this afternoon that Kate's mind whirled with the events. Not only had Mr. Adams kissed her, he had also stormed away when she brought up the subject of Melody and Drew. Moments ago, he angrily confronted her with her decision to allow Drew to befriend Calvin.

A tendril of guilt twisted through Kate's heart. If the truth were known, she owed Mr. Adams an apology as well. She should have never allowed him to kiss her. She should have never broached the subject of Drew's parentage after the kiss. That was none of her business, just as he had so skillfully pointed out. No wonder McCall stormed away. Kate probably would have done the same. And she really *didn't* have the authority to approve Drew's friendship with Calvin, even though she believed it was in Drew's best interest to have a friend.

Kate looked down at her fingers, tightly intertwined. "You aren't the only one who should be apologizing," she whispered. "I'm sorry for everything, too."

She heard McCall turn from the window but didn't dare look up. She felt him staring at her but didn't dare meet his gaze. She understood his amazement but didn't dare express her own. For despite their quarrels, Kate still felt dangerously drawn to McCall. She didn't trust herself not to run into his arms, place her hands on either side of his face, and tell him she would do her best to make the pain in his life go away. That danger, coupled with the knowledge that she shouldn't leave, no matter what her common sense demanded, would make looking at McCall emotionally hazardous.

"Does that mean you'll stay? Drew likes you so much. He would be disappointed if you—"

"And would you be disappointed?" For the second time that day, Kate covered her lips with trembling fingertips and studied the tips of her black ankle boots, peeking from beneath the hem of her green skirt. Why did she persist in saying things she shouldn't? How many times in one day would her face heat with embarrassment?

This was beyond unreasonable.

She was beyond mortified.

If her mother had witnessed Kate's behavior today, she would faint from embarrassment. Actually, her mother would not be pleased with Kate's behavior since her arrival in Dogwood. Perhaps part of Kate's straying from her mother's instructions stemmed from the fact that her mother was not present. Kate, for the first time in her life, was feeling free. Free to be herself. Even Zachary himself had admired Kate for her cool restraint. Kate thought that was simply who she was. But given a few weeks as a tutor, a few weeks in the presence of this man who looked like an aristocrat, who rode horses like a prince, who had known enough grief for two lifetimes, the man who still scrutinized her, after but a few weeks in the presence of McCall Adams, Kate was learning she was far from a woman of cool dignity. She was a woman of deep passions.

Without another word, McCall stepped out of the room and snapped the door shut behind him.

Kate released a pent-up breath and collapsed in the desk's chair. Her cold hands shaking, she covered her equally chilled face. At first, the hot tears silently trickled down her cheeks. But at last, she broke with the intensity of her emotions to produce a cross between a cough and a sob.

Once more, Kate heard the door open, someone step in, and the door closing behind him. Assuming Mr. Adams was returning, she stifled her cries, part from dread, part from expectation.

"Miss Lowell?"

Drew's hesitant voice produced a wave of relief in Kate that left her slumping. She nervously fished in her skirt's hidden pocket for the ever-present lace handkerchief. Gently, Kate dabbed away the tears and turned to face Drew. "Yes, Drew?" she said, producing a wobbly smile she was far from feeling.

"Is everything. . .are you—Dad. . .was he terribly mean to you?"

A new tear trickled from the corner of Kate's eye as she took in the deep concern cloaking Drew's every feature. The boy truly cared for Kate. How could she have ever thought of leaving him? He needed her. God had called her to this place at this time to minister to this Indian boy, just as He had called her to help that Indian girl in El Paso—the girl on which she had turned her back. Kate could not repeat that act, regardless of her differences with Mr. Adams.

"Your father apologized, Drew."

"But the whole thing was *my* fault." Drew hurried to Kate's side, gripped her hands, and knelt beside her.

"Oh Drew. . ."

"I should have never made you promise to hide my friendship with Calvin," he rushed. "I did it because I knew Dad would never approve, not after my fight with Calvin and the things his father said in town that day."

With a weary sigh, Kate stroked Drew's shiny, dark hair. "It's all right."

"Miss Lowell, please tell me you aren't going to leave. I would miss you so much!"

"Drew. . .Drew. . .Drew. . ." Kate crooned, standing and tugging on the boy's hands. He stood with her and she was once more stricken by how much he was growing. Drew was now as tall as Kate. "What makes you think I'm leaving?"

"It's obvious," Drew said, turning his intense gaze toward her shawl and the note she had barely started.

"You don't miss a thing, do you?" Kate said on a dry chuckle.

"No. Does that bother you?"

She turned to grip one of the straight-backed chairs near the fireplace and gazed out the window, toward the horse pasture. There, Mr. Adams trudged as if he were dragging one of the surrounding Texas hills behind him. "No. It doesn't bother me in the least," she said absently. "I'm thrilled to know I have such an keen student."

"So are you going to leave?"

"No, Drew. I'll be staying."

He remained respectfully silent, and Kate watched Mr. Adams until he was beyond her view. For the first time she realized just how much Drew needed a mother, just how much Mr. Adams needed a wife, regardless of what he said.

And Kate was forced to ask herself a question. Why had God placed her, a socialite, on this remote horse farm outside a tiny east Texas town? Did He have plans for her that went far beyond tutoring Drew?

Well, Lord, if You do, she prayed silently, *You are going to have to make some changes in me. . .and Mr. Adams.*

For Kate truly saw herself in that reflective moment in a way she never had before. McCall Adams wasn't the only one who needed to put his past pain behind him. She had told him only moments ago that he didn't have time for a life of his own because of his hold on Drew. The irony of Kate's own words haunted her, for she was guilty of the very thing of which she accused Mr. Adams. Kate was so busy holding onto her memory of Zachary that she was afraid to move forward in her own life.

Surely, Kate believed that God Himself was faced with a challenging task. For in her human view, she saw no way to remove her hold on Zachary, or Mr. Adams' hold on his deceased wife. . .and Drew.

"What do you know about my mother and my true. . . true father?" Drew muttered.

Kate, lost in her own thoughts, was jolted back to the present. She turned to face Drew, her eyes wide. "Wh–what?" she stammered, more as a means to stall for time than a need for Drew to repeat the question.

"I was wondering if you knew about. . .about my birth." Drew, his face flushed, crammed fidgeting hands into the pockets of his blue jeans.

Speechless, Kate grappled with any words she might say. She had only discovered the truth that day herself. She knew only the barest details. How could she explain the delicate situation to a fourteen-year-old boy? Furthermore, admitting to Drew that she knew his circumstances, only heightened her growing embarrassment. At long last, she said, "Drew, I. . .I think your father would be the best one to. . .to answer those questions. Don't you?" She laid an assuring hand on the boy's arm.

Silently, he nodded. "Ah. . .I guess," Drew said in resignation. "I just feel. . . uncomfortable. . . ." With a shrug, he helplessly looked into Kate's eyes.

"I understand," she reassured. "I think he feels the same way."

❧

"So why is it that you keep on bein' late finishin' your chores?" Eugene Wilcox paced the plank house's narrow front porch. He wasn't sure whether to beat the boy or give him a tongue-lashing. Calvin stood on the edge of the porch, his head hanging like a guilty dog. Eugene, arms folded, paused beside the rickety porch swing and brooded about Calvin's lack of responsibility. For the last three days, Nadine hadn't been able to start supper on time because Calvin was so late with the afternoon milking.

"I've been playing at the river," Calvin muttered.

"By yourself?"

Silence. The kind of silence that tells a father that there was someone else at the river. Eugene started thinking about all the neighboring farms and which property owners had children. At last, he remembered that the river served as a boundary between his land and McCall Adams' land. The possibilities of his son meeting an Indian turned Eugene's stomach.

"Have you been sneakin' off to see that stinkin' Injun boy?" Eugene demanded, hoping Calvin would deny the question.

"Yes sir," he muttered, fidgeting with the snap on the front of his overalls.

"I don't know what to think of you!" Eugene exploded.

Calvin jumped.

"One minute that Injun attacks you and smears the Wilcox name, and the next minute the two of ya are as close as twin pups."

"But Drew didn't start that fight in town," Calvin mumbled. "*I* started it."

Eugene's stomach burned with new anger. "Now you're startin' to lie to me! I saw that fight! I know that Injun started it!"

"No, Pa." Calvin looked up. "*I* did. Drew was just defendin' himself."

With the sound of a woodpecker furiously hammering

against a tree, Eugene silently observed his son. The sincere tone and honest gleam in Calvin's eyes confounded him. Usually, when the boy rebelled against Eugene's word, he did it with underhanded meanness. The last few weeks, there was definitely something unusual about Calvin. He had been more truthful and less rebellious. More kind and less hostile, even when Eugene himself had been hostile.

Eugene's thoughts of beating Calvin for befriending that "stinkin' Injun" left him. He was so stricken by his own son's blatant honesty, even in the face of punishment, that his anger slowly turned to amazement.

"Go on and finish your chores," Eugene growled. "And you won't be goin' to that river no time soon. Do you hear me?" Eugene yelled the last few words, right in the boy's face, to emphasize his earnestness. Even if he didn't beat the boy, at least Calvin would know he was close to getting a good one.

"Yes. . .yes. . .I hear ya, Pa," Calvin said, cringing as if he suspected a blow to follow.

"Please. . .please, don't. . ." a whiny voice said from the doorway.

Eugene turned to see his scrawny, blond wife. Her weak, blue eyes pleaded with him to leave the boy alone. Nadine's interference almost made Eugene want to reverse his decision not to take the boy to the woodshed. "Get back in that house and take care of the baby, woman!" he snarled.

The door instantly snapped shut.

"And you. . ." He turned back to Calvin. "Go milk the cow like I done told you to do."

Calvin rushed from his spot on the edge of the porch

and ran toward the cow pasture where one of the cows bellowed about her need for relief.

After a long day's work in the fields, Eugene's back ached. He slumped onto the ancient porch swing and its weathered slats creaked with his weight. His eyes narrowed as he watched Calvin, milk pail in hand, scramble through the rusty barbed-wire fence, and then lead the restless cow toward the barn. Something was mighty different about that boy of late. He was even gentler with the cows. It was enough to make Eugene want to ask him a few questions. But he could never afford to do that. *He's the boy and I'm the man. That's the way it's gonna stay.*

But respectful or not, if Calvin ever met that "stinkin' Indian" again, Eugene would beat the living daylights out of his son. Then, he would go find that Indian boy and beat the living daylights out of him as well. That Drew Adams had yet to pay for whipping Calvin in front of all of Dogwood. No matter who started the fight, Calvin got the worst end of it, and Drew had it coming to him.

Eugene smiled with satisfaction as a new thought struck him. *Just supposing Calvin tried to meet that Indian again at the river. . .and just supposing I were to find them together. . .that would give me the perfect opportunity to give both the boys a good thrashing.* Eugene rubbed his fist against his palm. He would start with the Indian. When Eugene got through with Drew Adams, he'd never again think he was good enough to associate with white folks.

eight

December marched on, and the chilly days became frigid. By mid-January, a light snowfall covered all of east Texas and kept the countryside frozen for one day. On the morning of the snow, Bob Mosely failed to appear to escort Kate to the horse farm. This in no way surprised Kate. By the next morning, Kate had developed a slight cold and sent word to the hotel receptionist to explain to Mr. Mosely that she was ill and would not be accompanying him to the horse farm.

After several hours in bed, Kate at last arose to discover that, perhaps, her cold would be a light one. Now bored and restless, she wondered if she should have gone with Mr. Mosely today after all.

Nonetheless, the snow and her slight illness had given Kate a much-needed break. As she stood at her hotel window and looked over the surrounding hills, lightly dusted with the melting white powder, she breathed deeply and relaxed—truly relaxed—for the first time in weeks. She wasn't at the horse farm yesterday. She wouldn't go today. Tomorrow was Saturday. That meant by Monday, Kate would have four days away from the inner tension that surfaced each time she saw McCall Adams.

Since the day he kissed her, Kate felt as if her nerves were on razor's edge. Monday through Friday, the whole time she was at the horse ranch, Kate spent every spare moment looking over her shoulder or out the schoolroom's window. Part in fear. Part in expectation. She desperately wanted to see McCall—yet desperately wanted to avoid him. Drew, seemingly oblivious to her plight, had turned into a model student. Other than occasional distant glimpses of the boy's father, Kate would have assumed she and Drew were alone on that expansive ranch. Nevertheless, she felt as if McCall were standing behind her each second, investigating her every move.

Absently, Kate turned her attention toward the streets of Dogwood. At daybreak yesterday, the streets had seemed covered in a magical, white veil. Today, the rutted roads appeared to be full of muddy, trampled cotton, marred beyond use. Yesterday few people came in from the countryside, but today the town teamed with people. The weak sunshine filtering through gray, blotchy clouds promised to warm the temperatures enough to completely melt the dissipating snow by noon.

Yesterday, Kate had stayed the day in her hotel room to begin reading *Pride and Prejudice*, sent by her mother. She also caught up on her correspondence with her mother and two sisters, who all begged her to return to El Paso. Kate could never explain to them why she continued to stay. Certainly, it wasn't for the forty dollars a month McCall paid her. Given her family's financial security, they would never understand her very deep need to help others, and Kate wasn't even sure if helping Drew was the only reason she was staying. Therefore, she simply ignored her family's written pleas and responded with news of the good time she was having.

After finishing yesterday's correspondence, Kate had even spent the afternoon napping, but a recurring, disturbing nightmare kept waking her. Kate had once more been dreaming she stood on the middle of the tree trunk, fallen across a river. Zachary, in ethereal form, hovered on one side of the riverbank. McCall occupied the opposite bank. A ghost-like beauty, sobbing uncontrollably, clung to McCall and placed a newborn baby into his arms. Kate's heart pounded in sympathy for the crying woman. Wanting to comfort Melody, she ran across the tree trunk, planning to wrap her arms around the broken girl. Kate almost reached the bank when she lost her balance. She began waving her arms, flailing in the air, feeling the tug of the rushing river beneath her. Kate repeatedly screamed for McCall's help, but he never even acknowledged her cries. He only clung to Melody. She twisted to beseech Zachary's assistance, but he faded from view. At last Kate tumbled toward the river to be caught by Drew who asked her why he was part Indian, then he immediately begged her to become his mother. At this point, Kate awoke with a start, just as she had every night for the last month. As always, she was drenched in sweat. Her heart beat furiously, and she gasped for air.

Wanting to expunge the troubling dream from her mind, she turned from the window and peered across her small room. Already, the morning was half over, and Kate felt as if the walls were closing in on her. With a delicate sneeze, she plopped onto the bed's blue and beige patchwork coverlet and looked toward the wardrobe's half-opened door. In that cedar closet hung her few dresses, which Kate wore over and over again while tutoring Drew. When she came to Dogwood, Kate never anticipated she would be here so long. She had purchased only one gingham dress, which she now wore. Her few other dresses were much too formal, but Kate had been forced to wear them.

Kate drew a decisive breath. Suddenly, she stood and reached for her reticule and shawl, which lay on the end of the bed. Kate would make another trip to the dressmaker's. She could certainly use two more work dresses, and today presented the perfect chance for her to place her order.

But first, she would stop by the general store to mail the letters to her mother and sisters. She grabbed the envelopes lying on the small, oval table in the corner and whisked into the hallway. Within minutes, Kate picked her way across the street, full of muddy slush, and opened the door to the Dogwood General store. The smells of coffee, peppermint, and new material greeted her. Kate glanced around the store, lined with horse plows, bags of cornmeal, sugar, flour, and the ever-present wall of postal boxes behind the counter. Immediately she was drawn to the material table and began examining several bolts of heavy cotton, exactly the kind of material she needed for an all-purpose work dress. Out of the corner of her eye, Kate noticed the buxom Bess Tucker about to approach her, but she stopped to help another couple, buying supplies for their kitchen.

At closer observation, Kate noticed the couple was Travis Campbell and his new wife, Rachel. Never in her life had Kate wanted so desperately to disappear as that moment. She suppressed the urge to crawl under the material table, but decided to simply keep her back to them in hopes that they wouldn't notice her. The last time she saw Travis and Rachel, she and Travis broke off their engagement and she rode away, leaving him to marry the woman of his heart, Rachel Isaacs. That was the day before Kate met Mr. Adams and Drew at the train station.

To encounter Travis and Rachel now was highly awkward and embarrassing. Kate didn't even know if they were aware she was still in Dogwood. At last, she decided to simply turn around and leave without mailing the letters. She would go to the dressmaker's, who usually kept material in stock, and return to mail the letters after ordering her dress. Kate whirled around to bump squarely into Rachel.

"Oh excuse me," the young redhead said politely. "I didn't realize you. . ." She trailed off as she recognized exactly who she had bumped into—her husband's former fiancée. "Miss Lowell!" she said with faint surprise.

"Mrs. Campbell," Kate said calmly, feeling anything *but* calm. She stole a glance toward Travis, tall and fair, as he neared. The last time she saw him they were on friendly, although strained, terms. Kate was very much at peace about their mutual decision to break the engagement, but she hoped Mrs. Campbell in no way thought Kate was pining for Travis.

"Hello, Kate," Travis said as he neared. "We heard you were still in town; it's a delight to see you."

"Yes. . ." Kate cleared her throat and produced a shy smile. "I suppose there isn't much that goes on in Dogwood that everyone doesn't know about."

Rachel released a spontaneous giggle, and Kate eased a bit. Perhaps the flush on Mrs. Campbell's cheeks was an indicator of her happiness *and* security in her marriage.

Helplessly searching for any topic of conversation, Kate opened her mouth and heard herself say, "The snow must have made you as restless as it did me. I decided that after being trapped inside yesterday I needed to get out today."

"Actually, we—Rachel needed to see Dr. Engle," Travis

said, placing an arm around his wife's waist as if she were a fragile doll.

The glowing, adoring gaze Rachel threw Travis left the rest unsaid. She was most likely expecting their first child. Kate shot a furtive glanced toward Rachel's waist-line only to find it unaltered. Perhaps Mrs. Campbell was very early in her pregnancy. Kate furtively hoped there were no problems.

Rachel turned her attention back to Kate. "Travis and I were thinking of sending you an invitation to dine with us one evening if—"

"That is so thoughtful of you," Kate interrupted. "But I'm so busy with the tutoring that I—"

"We understand," Travis said. And Kate knew Travis well enough to interpret the gleam in his green eyes. Such a meeting would be as uncomfortable for him as for Kate. Surprisingly, his young wife seemed the most at ease with the whole situation.

"Well, it was extremely nice to see you again," Kate said in her most refined tone.

Fully prepared to gracefully exit the store, she curtsied and began walking toward the front door. But it would appear that Kate had no room for escape this day, from any situation. For when she was no more than ten feet from the doorway, it swung open and McCall Adams walked into the store. Kate trembled in astonishment. Behind her stood the man she had once agreed to marry; and in front of her stood the man she would probably dream about the rest of her life but would never marry.

Kate would have loved to pretend she didn't see McCall, but that proved impossible, for he looked straight at her. The purposeful gleam in his dark eyes proclaimed that he had found the person for whom he was looking.

"Miss Lowell," he said with a slight smile. "The hotel owner mentioned that you might be here. May I have a minute of your time, please?"

"Yes, of course," Kate said quietly. She cringed, imagining that every eye in the store must be fixed on her as she stepped onto the boardwalk with Mr. Adams. Yet a quick glance over her shoulder proved no one watched her departure. Bess Tucker hovered near Rachel and Travis as they joyfully examined a tiny bonnet, just the size to fit a baby. The two most certainly were expectant parents.

As Mr. Adams shut the door behind them, Kate's heart twisted with a longing she thought had been obliterated by Zachary's death. The longing to be a mother. To hold a helpless infant in her arms and know the tiny baby belonged to her and would one day return her love. A stab of envy, as quick as a sword, passed through Kate's heart. Would she ever know the kind of joy Rachel exuded?

She seemed forever destined to love men who could never return her love. Zachary now lay cold in his grave. And McCall Adams, was she falling in love with McCall? Kate had guarded herself against the possibility from the onset of their acquaintance. Yet standing here beside him on this cold January day, looking up into his velvet brown eyes, so full of pain, soaking in every detail of him, Kate began to wonder if she was on the road to forgetting Zachary and losing her heart to McCall. Their kiss—that earth shattering kiss—she had relived it a million times. And each time, her heart pounded as if she had run to west Texas.

Still silent, McCall gently took her elbow and steered

her out of the door's way. Kate resisted the urge to jerk her tingling arm out of his grasp, and simultaneously she resisted the urge to fall into his arms. Wondering why he had come for her, Kate stole another glance at McCall and found him appraising her. Before she realized what she was doing, Kate reached up with the intent to stroke the feather-like lines around his eyes and the softness of his dark beard. But she stopped herself and instead, covered her lips with her fingertips.

Why was he even here? He seemed somewhat unsure of himself, and Kate almost exploded with the mounting tension. Unable to withstand another second of his probing gaze, she spoke at last. "You wanted to see me for something, Mr. Adams?"

"Yes. Actually, I did. I. . ." He stopped to clear his throat. "I came into town after Mr. Mosely informed me that you were unavailable this morning to ride to the ranch with him. He seemed to be under the impression that you were going to. . ." McCall trailed off meaningfully, as a glimmer of relief danced through his eyes

Did he think that she had plans not to return to her tutoring position? The thought barely had time to form before Kate produced a high-pitched sneeze. "Excuse me. I seem to have developed a slight cold." She dabbed the end of her nose with her lace handkerchief.

"I'm so sorry. I didn't know. Is this the reason you left word for Mr. Mosely that you wouldn't be coming?"

"I told the hotel maid to tell the receptionist that I was ill. That apparently was not the message Mr. Mosely received. Please forgive me."

"You have nothing to apologize for. There simply must have been some miscommunication. Mr. Mosely was under the impression that you. . .well. . .that you wouldn't be coming back *ever*."

"Mr. Adams, do you honestly think I would do such a thing without notifying you?"

"Were you planning to notify me before?" One dark brow arched in an almost flirting manner, and Kate's heart palpitated despite herself.

"I. . .I. . .was at least going to leave a note for Drew, and you would have understood from that note. . . ." She examined the top button of his pullover denim shirt as pedestrians bustled around them and horses and wagons sloshed through the muddy streets.

"I hope you understand, Miss Lowell, just how much I have come to depend on you on behalf of Drew."

"Only for Drew?" the words seemed to have been snatched from her tongue, and Kate covered her lips with her gloved fingertips. Her heart felt as if it dropped to her feet. Kate longed to race back to her hotel room, bury her face in the depths of her feather bed, and die from embarrassment. "I'm so sorry," she rushed. "I don't know what comes over me when I'm speaking with you, Mr. Adams." She refused to look into his eyes. Instead, Kate addressed the door to the dressmaker's just across the street. "I seem to be forever saying things I don't. . .I shouldn't. . ." Another dainty sneeze. "If you'll please excuse me, I think I should return to my room now."

Kate whirled away from McCall and hurried along the covered boardwalk. At the corner, she began running across the street, almost tripping as her skirt dragged against the mounds of mud and snow that the wagons had created as they sliced through the slush. Only when she reached the boardwalk in front of her hotel did she hear

Mr. Adams calling.

"Miss Lowell! Miss Lowell, wait!"

Pretending she didn't hear, Kate whipped open the hotel door, stepped into the quaint lobby, and rushed to the receptionist's desk. "I must b–be alone," she said, panting for breath. "Please tell any c–callers that I–I'm unavailable." Another sneeze punctuated her request.

"Of course, ma'am," the elderly lady replied.

Kate, hearing the door open behind her, hurled herself toward the dark, wooden stairway.

"Miss Lowell, we must talk!"

McCall's voice stopped Kate mid-stride. How could she ever pretend she didn't hear him now?

nine

Eugene Wilcox noticed Calvin missing a good hour before he went looking for him. The boy was supposed to be doing his chores, not playing at the river. Eugene crunched through the woods, noticing that the last of yesterday's snowfall was melting. Deep in his gut, he knew Calvin had disobeyed him and had gone to meet that worthless Indian at the river again. He gripped the horsewhip all the tighter. Once Eugene got through with that Indian, he wouldn't be fit to meet the devil himself. He spit a stream of tobacco against the trunk of a stately oak. His breath formed a white mist around his moist lips each time he exhaled.

This stupidity on Calvin's part really surprised Eugene. The boy had been exceptionally good of late, even good enough to make Eugene suspicious at first. But during the last week, he had begun to wonder if Calvin's recent church attendance at that church up the road had anything to do with his good behavior. Last Sunday, he had even asked Eugene and Nadine to go with him. Eugene had growled that Nadine was busy with the baby and he needed the rest. Calvin had silently left their three-room home, and Eugene felt as if the boy had touched his heart.

The odd moment left Eugene wishing he could handle his son the way he saw other men treating their boys. The truth was that Eugene couldn't quite do it. He didn't know what to do with Calvin other than give the boy the same treatment he had received as a kid. Grabbing a bare vine, Eugene angrily ripped it away from his path. If the truth were known, Calvin got far fewer beatings than Eugene ever got. He remembered after one particular beating, he could hardly walk for a week. And his right ankle had never been the same since his pa kicked him so hard that day.

Eugene's stomach turned with the memory. By the time he left home, he hated his father. Thinking of beating Calvin today almost made Eugene wish he had not been disobedient. Lately, Eugene had heard Calvin praying for him. Even though Wilcox had no desire to be affected, he could not deny the influence.

Despite those bothersome prayers, somebody needed a beating over this business of Calvin meeting that Indian even if was only the Indian who got it. From the little he knew of God, Eugene supposed He didn't take too kindly to a couple of scheming boys.

At last, the roar of the narrow river met Eugene's ears. Next, the smell of fresh water. Eugene crept closer until he saw the frothy water, fifteen feet below, rushing across the protruding, flat rocks. A canopy of trees blocked out the weak, winter sun and the air around the river was some-what colder. Just as Eugene figured, Calvin and the Indian sat side by side on a big rock not twenty feet away. Eugene cringed with the thought of his clean, white son allowing a nasty Indian to even breathe close to him. He wrinkled his nose in disgust and poised to jump on that no-account kid and give him the beating of his life.

But the words those two boys shared wafted toward Eugene over the sound of the river and stilled his attack.

"You've done told me so much, Drew," Calvin said. "If it weren't for you, I'd a never gotten to know God, not for real. Why *can't* you come to church with me?"

"Because my Dad says I can't. We don't go to church. We worship at home on Sundays by ourselves."

"But the Good Book says you're supposed to go to church!" Calvin held up the black book that Eugene had seen him reading the last few weeks.

"I know." Drew stood. "But Dad says it's best for us to stay home mostly."

"Do you think it's because of what you said the other day—that you found out you're part Injun?"

Drew, turning his back on Calvin, shrugged his shoulders. "Your father doesn't seem to like me too much because of that. I guess maybe there's more like him." The sound of the river almost blotted out Drew's words.

Eugene knew now was the time for him to jump in the middle of those boys and teach them a lesson. He gripped the horsewhip, raised it, and prepared to rush forward.

"Well, I guess I really need to get back to my chores," Calvin said, standing. "I don't want to disappoint my pa. I've been doin' what you said and praying for him and trying to be good. . .even when he's mean."

Eugene's stomach twisted in guilt. What Calvin was saying was absolutely true. Why was Eugene constantly, compulsively, treating Calvin just like his father treated him? Deep, deep inside, Eugene sometimes wanted things to be different. But it seemed the harder he tried, the meaner he got with Calvin, and that only made Calvin meaner—until lately. Did that black book Calvin held have anything to do with the change in the boy? If there really was a God, *did* Calvin know him like he said he did?

His thoughts spinning, Eugene silently watched as the boys exchanged a series of handshakes and ended with a little childish chant that mentioned brotherhood and God. Then Drew rushed across the fallen tree to jump onto the opposite bank, and Calvin turned to race up the pathway leading toward their home.

Eugene, deep in thought, barely noticed when the whip slipped from his grasp.

੨๋

McCall momentarily thought Miss Lowell was pausing long enough for him to approach her. But he no more took two steps forward, when she began running up the stairs as if another moment in his presence would choke her. Yet McCall knew beyond doubt that wasn't the case. The open admiration flowing from her eyes only moments before, the instant he had been almost sure she was going to stroke his face, even her own words attested to Miss Lowell's growing attachment to him.

The truth of the matter was that McCall's heart had almost stopped the instant Mr. Mosely relayed his erroneous message that Kate would not be returning. McCall had tried to maintain his distance from Kate over the past weeks. He had tried to guard his heart against any threat of her influence. He had desperately tried to maintain a grip on his memory of Melody. He had pleaded with God to release him from his growing feelings for Miss Lowell. But only one thought circled through his mind in answer to his prayers:

Release the past.

As he watched Kate ascend to the top of the stairway, McCall decided to go after her. Taking the steps two at a time, he called her once more. "Miss Lowell. . .*please*. . . may I have a few more moments of your time?"

"Excuse me, Sir!" the aging receptionist called in a

squawking voice. "We don't allow male callers upstairs with our lady guests. It isn't appropriate!"

Ignoring her, McCall reached Miss Lowell's side and gripped her upper arm. "Please give me a few more moments," he said softly.

Kate muffled a broken sob, and McCall saw rivulets of tears dampening her cheeks. "Please allow me the honor of going to my room and dying of embarrassment in dignity, Mr. McCall," she mumbled. A furious sneeze followed her tearful words, and she refused to look him in the eyes.

With a fond chuckle, McCall removed his handkerchief from his pant's pocket and gently stroked away her tears.

"I don't know what possesses me to say the things I do when I am with you. Please accept my most humble apologies and my pledge to never speak to you again as long as I live."

The receptionist, now standing at the base of the stairs, cleared her throat meaningfully.

McCall shot an impatient glance toward her then turned back to Kate. "I can accept your apology, but I must resist your pledge to never speak to me again. That would be highly impractical, don't you think, considering your position as my son's tutor?"

"Sir, I'm afraid that I must demand your returning to the lobby," the old lady insisted. "Or I will be forced to send for my son, who happens to be the owner."

Kate looked toward the receptionist and McCall followed suit. He felt Kate's indecision, whether to return to her room or go to the lobby with him.

"Please," McCall said, not certain of the wisdom in insisting upon Miss Lowell's company. He certainly was in no way ready to begin a long-term relationship with her. It wouldn't be fair to her. Melody still held him too tightly. Perhaps he should be completely honest with Kate and tell her that there was no hope in a relationship between them.

Nevertheless, McCall could no longer deny that Miss Lowell was more of a distraction for him than his willpower could endure. Proof of this stood in his rushing to town to insist she not leave her position, only to discover she had no intentions of doing so. If he were honest with himself, McCall would admit that he had begun to hunger for the briefest glimpses of her. The last time they spoke, she had asked him if he would be disappointed if she left. Only minutes before, she had asked him if his dependence on her was only for Drew. McCall should answer both of those questions and hopefully put to rest some of the torment in her eyes.

But regardless of his feelings for Miss Lowell, his heart would always belong to Melody. He needed to make certain Kate understood this. The time had come to be completely honest. If she were willing to share his heart, perhaps McCall would. . .what? This line of thought left him blinking in surprise.

At last Kate silently turned and began to descend the stairs once more.

Satisfied, the wrinkled receptionist stiffly returned to her duties at the front desk. McCall, his heart pounding out expectant beats, followed Miss Lowell and joined her on one of the green velvet settees in the hotel lobby. He glanced over his shoulder to see the receptionist watching them. He boldly held her gaze, and she abruptly turned to busy herself with paperwork.

"Please understand, Miss Lowell," he said softly. "That

I in no way scorn your questions and feel that, given my own behavior, they are most certainly appropriate."

"Really?" she said, tormenting the handkerchief in her hands.

"Of course. When a man. . .kisses a woman. . .it implies . . .and I most certainly feel that I have implied. . .and that you most certainly have every right to ask. . ." McCall groped for new words but found nothing except his own heightened emotions. Was he falling in love with Miss Lowell, despite his opposition? Desperately, he tried to recall the name of Drew's mother, long carved upon his heart, but his mind was so jumbled at the sight of the lovely Kate Lowell that her name momentarily escaped him.

"And when a woman allows a man to kiss her without. . . without so much as. . .as a commitment. . .it–it implies. . ." Still refusing to look at McCall, Kate stood and hurried to the floor-to-ceiling window that provided an expansive view of the streets of Dogwood.

McCall slowly followed her and stopped within inches of her back. His stomach churned as her hair, caught into its meticulous bun, glistened in the sunlight pouring through the window. What would it be like to awaken to her every morning of his life? *God save me, I am drowning!* he pleaded heavenward, feeling as if this situation with Miss Lowell were rapidly growing out of his own control. He lambasted himself for following the impulse to ride into town when Bob Mosely supplied the misinformation. McCall should have relied on logic and realized Miss Lowell wouldn't leave without bidding Drew good-bye. But he hadn't. He had acted on blind instinct and chased after the woman who—

"It implies. . ." Kate whispered haltingly. "You know

exactly what it implies. And. . .and given that, plus my humiliating questions, Mr. Adams, I have no other recourse but to believe you must think. . .y–you must think. . ." She gulped.

"I think nothing but. . ." He place his hand on her shoulder. "Would you marry me, Miss Lowell?"

"*What*?" She spun to face him, her cheeks decidedly paler than they had ever been.

McCall couldn't believe he had blurted such a question. He hadn't even prayed about it. But if the truth were known, McCall understood in the deepest recesses of his heart what God's will was on this subject. God was beckoning him to release the past and embrace the future with this lovely woman before him. But he had resisted the Lord, was even *now* resisting. For he knew with sickening truth that even if Miss Lowell did agreed to marry him, she would also have to assent to sharing his heart with Melody. What woman would ever consent to such a proposal. But would Kate have to know he still harbored a secret love for his former wife?

"What about Melody?" she whispered, as if she could read his thoughts.

"What about her?"

"You're still in love with her." Kate spoke the words as if she hoped he would refute them.

McCall helplessly stared into her eyes and knew he couldn't lie.

"Do you honestly think I would ever marry a man who was in love with another woman?" she asked, her whisper much louder than before, her cheeks now flushing.

He instinctively glanced toward the nosy receptionist to find her attention riveted to them as if she were straining to hear every word of their intense conversation. Caught in the act of eavesdropping, she guiltily rushed from the desk and through the nearby office doorway.

"Besides," Kate added with a weary echo to her words. "Even if you weren't still. . .still in love with Melody, I have my own misgivings." She studied her fidgeting, gloved hands.

"Are you talking about your experience with Zachary?" McCall asked gently, not certain if he was disappointed or relieved that Kate hadn't immediately accepted his spontaneous proposal.

Her head snapped up. Her eyes widened. Her lips parted in astonishment. "How do you know Zachary's name?"

"Dr. Engle told me about Zachary the first day I met you. If you remember, I dropped off Drew with him before you and I talked at Dotty's, and he mentioned. . ."

"That's something incredibly private. How would he know such about me?" she demanded, a frustrated note to her voice.

"He's like a father to Rachel Campbell, and she has shared with him the struggle her husband faced in forgiving himself for your fiancé's death."

"Dr. Engle certainly does know about everyone, doesn't he?" Kate snapped spitefully.

McCall narrowed his eyes and immediately jumped to the doctor's defense. "He never had any children, but he is like a father to several people in town, me included. The man is as good as gold."

"Yes, and as nosy as. . .as. . ." She sputtered to a stop and whirled to once more gaze out the window.

"He meant well," McCall said.

"Well, it's none of his business!"

"Or mine?" he asked, at last deeply aware that he wasn't

the only one with a former love that still haunted him. At once, McCall remembered Kate's urging him to release his own past and his hold on Drew. His gut twisted in irritation as he clearly saw what Dr. Engle could never know. Kate Lowell was still in love with her dead fiancé. How dare she preach to him when she harbored her own ghosts. "Miss Lowell," McCall said evenly, a note of aggravation in his voice. "I find it highly inconsiderate of you to point your finger at me about my. . .my feelings for Melody when you . . .you are guilty of the exact same predicament."

"How dare you!" she gasped, turning to face him once more. This time Kate's eyes snapped with abundant ire.

"I dare because *you* have dared!" McCall gripped her upper arms and wanted to kiss her again—kiss her until both Melody and Zachary were expunged from their hearts and Kate agreed to marry him. These new thoughts left him breathless. McCall, now within inches of her, peering deeply into her eyes, felt as if he would live forever in torment—desperately wanting to give his heart to Kate, yet unable to release Melody.

"Stop it! Stop it! Just–just stop it!" Twisting away from his hold, Kate raced toward the stairwell once more. This time, she hovered at the top, not because McCall beckoned her but because she had one last, surprising message to hurl toward him.

"I'm leaving. I'm going back home to El Paso. I cannot, I *will* not continue like this. Tell Drew I will not be back!" With a broken sob, she ran from sight.

ten

Three months later, Kate settled onto her chair in the ranch's schoolroom and reflected over the weeks since she had proclaimed her decision to leave Dogwood. Her resolve to leave had lasted until the Sunday after she hurled the words toward Mr. Adams. That Sunday in church, she had bowed her head and truly sought the Lord's guidance concerning her hasty decision. During those quiet moments on the church pew, Kate felt in her spirit that leaving her tutoring position would mean direct disobedience to God. Once more, God brought to her mind the incident with the Indian girl in the streets of El Paso. Once more, Kate felt that turning her back on Drew would be like refusing that helpless adolescent all over again.

So! Kate had hired a driver to escort her to the horse farm Monday morning. Although she never saw Mr. Adams that morning, Drew bounded out of the log cabin like a young buck and embraced her with his engaging smile. Once they settled in the schoolroom, he industriously turned his mind to studies. Later, Drew made only one vague reference to her supposed resignation, and Kate had simply stated the truth: She felt she had spoken too hastily and that, after praying about it, she knew resigning the position was not God's will. Whether or not Drew ever told his father this was still a mystery to Kate; she and McCall had not spoken since that day in the hotel lobby when he blurted that unexpected proposal.

Thoughts of that moment still left Kate speechless and appalled. The man must be half-crazy to think she would *ever* marry him when his heart still belonged to Melody! The fact that Mr. Adams found Kate attractive was not hidden. He had obviously expressed his attraction to her, but a marriage must be based on much more. Nevertheless, despite her astonishment at McCall's proposal, from that fateful moment when he proposed, Kate mused about what life would be like as McCall's wife, as Drew's mother. For God had already shown her that Drew desperately needed a mother. And McCall—McCall, despite his lingering love for Melody, desperately needed a wife.

But was Kate the one? The prospect left her reeling in confusion.

The schoolroom's door opened, and Kate swiveled, expecting Drew. An hour ago, she had sent him on a venture to gather the final bugs that would finish their spring collection. But instead of Drew, Kate encountered McCall's bland scrutiny.

Her heart pounded.

Her palms moistened.

Her lips trembled.

"Mr. Mosely and I needed another helping hand with the west fences. Where's Drew?" McCall asked as if they were on perfectly amiable terms.

"He's finishing the bug collection." Kate rasped in a strained voice. "He should be back in a few minutes."

"Thank you." He hesitated. "Are you certain he is no longer playing with Calvin Wilcox?"

"As certain as I can be," Kate said, a bit defensively. "When I allow him to explore the woods, he always comes back with the things for which I sent him within the allotted time. I haven't discussed it with him, but I assumed he understood your view on the subject."

McCall produced a curt nod. "How is your afternoon progressing today? Are the two of you on schedule?"

"Yes. We're actually ahead in our schedule by a few days," Kate said, her defensive tone increasing. She felt as if the man were interrogating her. Why would he arrive after a three-month silence and accost her with a barrage of questions?

"Good. Then if you don't mind his missing the afternoon, I'll go see if I can find him. We really need his help on the fences."

"He's your son, Mr. Adams," Kate said pointedly. "That's perfectly fine with me."

McCall narrowed his eyes as if her words irritated him.

Kate, determined to maintain a demeanor of wide-eyed innocence, didn't dare flinch away.

"I was simply trying to be polite. I in no way intended to offend you," he said firmly.

"I never said I was offended."

"No, but your words—" He took an impatient breath. "Never mind. If you would like Mr. Mosely to drive you back into town while I find Drew, I'll be perfectly happy to tell him."

"Am I in your way?" she asked, not knowing why she was suddenly bent on needling him.

"No. That was the farthest thing from my mind." He pushed his dark hat back from his brow as if his irritation were growing.

"Good. Then I'll stay until my normal hour of departure. I have several things to do here before leaving today."

"Fine," he snapped.

"Fine, then."

He turned as if to leave then swiveled to face her. "Miss Lowell," he said deliberately. "We haven't spoken in quite some time, but I must say that I think the same of you today as I thought of you the last time we spoke."

Automatically assuming Mr. Adams referred to his spontaneous proposal, Kate's face heated in surprise. "Mr. Adams, *please*, I—"

"You are beyond doubt the most exasperating woman I have ever met!"

Gaping, Kate stood, ready to do verbal battle. "Well, thank you for your kindness, Mr. Adams. I am certainly glad Drew doesn't agree with you."

"This has nothing to do with Drew."

"But my presence does."

"Undoubtedly! And if it weren't for Drew, I'd. . ."

"You'd what?" she challenged.

He eyed her silently.

"You'd send me back to El Paso? Is that it?"

"I never said that!" McCall stepped outside and slammed the door before she had a chance to form another thought.

Kate plopped back into her chair, resisting the urge to run after McCall Adams and explain to him that *he* was the most exasperating man *she* had ever met. And she wanted to make certain he understood that the only thing keeping her in Dogwood was Drew. Kate furiously counted the weeks until school would be over. Exactly six. If she could last six weeks, she could return to El Paso for the summer. From there, she could decide whether or not she would return to Dogwood in the fall. If McCall requested her decision now, Kate would deliver a firm "no."

But would that be God's will?

With a groan, she rested her elbows on the desk and covered her face with her hands. It always came back to that one conflict. Her human side wanted to bolt, while God consistently tugged her back to tutoring Drew.

"Why are you doing this to me?" she prayed, but received only silence.

Wanting to ease her frazzled nerves, Kate reached for her Bible and scooted the oil lamp closer. The bright spring sunshine flooded through the windows, but Kate still needed the extra lamplight to read the fine print. The time she allowed Drew to explore in the woods was usually the time she spent in the Word of God. She desperately needed a soothing Psalm today. But the Bible plopped open to the spot where Zachary's dried red rose resided. She encountered the rose every time she opened her Bible. Up until a few weeks ago, Kate always paused to ponder the man of her heart. But this afternoon, with the kerosene lamp producing fluttering shadows across the pages of her Bible, she realized many days had passed since she reflected over her time with Zachary. She picked up the flattened flower and studied it. Her nerves still scattered from her encounter with McCall, Kate stroked the lifeless petals, and one flaked away to float toward the Bible's opened pages.

Kate reflected over her last evening with Zachary.

She thought about his funeral.

She recalled the hours she had grieved his loss.

Surprisingly, no tears formed in her eyes. Only a dull ache remained in her heart. A sweet, dull ache. A nuance of the love Kate had once cherished, then lost. She glanced down at the pages of her Bible, now marked by the pale traces of the rose. And one verse from Luke, the words of

Jesus himself, sprang up at her: "The Spirit of the Lord is upon me, because he hath anointed me to preach the gospel to the poor; he hath sent me to heal the broken-hearted, to preach deliverance to the captives, and recovering of sight to the blind, to set at liberty them that are bruised."

"Oh Lord," Kate whispered as her eyes misted. "Can it be that You are healing my broken heart? Are You trying to set me at liberty?"

Release the past.

As those three words whisked through Kate's mind, she yearned for the strength and ability to embrace her future. No more hanging onto the memory of a man she could never again touch. No more living in fear of once more losing a love. No more resisting the divine will of God for her life.

But could Kate truly do it? Could she truly obey God's bidding and release the past?

With new determination, she pressed her lips together, picked up the rose, and walked toward the fireplace. Now that April was in full bloom, Drew seldom built fires. However, this morning had proven cool enough for a fire, but there was now no sign of live coals. Kate reached for the poker and stirred the gray ashes. A few coals glowed to life. She replaced the poker and brushed the dried rose petals against her lips.

Dare she burn the last flower Zachary had given her?

❧

McCall stormed across the north pasture toward the path that Drew always used when scouting the woods. Even though McCall searched for Drew, his mind remained with Kate Lowell. She knew how to goad him as no other woman had ever goaded him. McCall had thought, he honestly thought, that there would be no harm in simply opening the door of the summer kitchen and inquiring after Drew.

He hadn't spoken to Miss Lowell in the three months since their tense conversation in the hotel lobby. And for three months McCall had wanted to rip out his own tongue. How could he have ever proposed to her? Several times he had hoped that the whole episode was nothing more than a bad dream, only to discover the dreadful truth. McCall had not been dreaming. He had indeed proposed to Miss Lowell.

Nonetheless, when Kate declared that she would not return to tutor Drew, McCall felt as if a part of him were dying. So convinced was he of her intent, he even told Drew she would not be back. When Kate arrived as usual that next Monday morning, McCall didn't know whether to sing with glee or groan with embarrassment. But from the moment he saw Miss Lowell step from the hired carriage and into the schoolroom, McCall had vowed to avoid her.

Why, oh why, did he break that vow? If not for Drew's love for Kate, McCall would politely dismiss her. She only brought misery to his already tortured heart. One part of him declared lifelong allegiance to Melody while something deep within urged him to release the woman whom had clung to him unto death. But McCall had determined it was impossible to release Melody. He was but a mere human being, and some things were unfeasible for a man to do.

With these thoughts plaguing him, McCall entered the woods, which were filled with wild dogwoods and the sounds of spring. He had precious little time to think of

Miss Lowell. He needed to find Drew and head back to the fence line.

During the last months, Drew had seemingly adhered to McCall's request to avoid Calvin Wilcox, but McCall had a tiny doubt in the back of his mind. Drew was normally a good, obedient boy, but lately he seemed to be testing several of the rules that McCall had set for him. Why would the rule about Calvin be any different?

As he continued to crunch through the woods, McCall began calling his son. His heart was truly troubled with the battles the two of them had faced of late. It would seem that something very deep was troubling Drew, and he would not tell McCall. This was so strange to McCall, for Drew and he had always been the best of friends. McCall had, by some miraculous design, been able to keep the balance between his authority as a father and Drew's need for a friend. But lately, Drew seemed miles away from McCall. Several times, he wanted to approach Miss Lowell about the issue, but had refrained. McCall hated to draw her any closer to the family than she already was. As things stood, McCall was just barely able to keep her at arm's length. Any further interaction and he couldn't trust himself not to collapse at her feet and again beg her to marry him.

But what insanity! She would never marry him as long he loved Melody. McCall had begun to think the love for his deceased wife would haunt him until death. For the first time, he entertained the longing to release it.

"Drew!" he called again through his cupped hands. "Drew!"

McCall continued traipsing through the woods, instinctively winding his way toward the river. He truly hoped he didn't find Drew and Calvin together. McCall had not punished Drew when he first found out about the friendship. But at this point, if Drew were willingly disobeying McCall, he would have no choice.

"Drew!" he bellowed again as the sound of the river skipped along the newly budding trees.

"Dad! Dad! Come quick!"

The faint, panicked call, almost indiscernible, left McCall's heart racing in dread. He hurled himself forward, racing toward the sound of his son's troubled voice.

"Drew! Where are you!"

"Down here!"

With the river now in clear view, McCall looked over the steep bank and toward Drew's voice. The boy stood beside a body crumpled limply at his feet—the body of Calvin Wilcox.

"It's Calvin, Dad! It's Calvin! He fell off the log, and. . . and. . ."

His stomach churning, McCall glanced toward the fallen tree, which he had warned Drew about when he found him and Calvin walking across it in December. Beneath the fallen tree, the river swirled at one of its deepest levels. Even though he had assumed Calvin could swim as well as Drew, McCall had insisted both the boys stay off the precarious log.

He skidded down the sandy bank, not knowing what to expect. Was Calvin drowned?

eleven

Eugene Wilcox, plowing in the north pasture, stopped in his tracks when he heard Nadine's distraught cries.

"Eugene! Eugene! It's Calvin! Eugene! Something terrible has happened!"

His heart felt as if it dropped to his knees. Forgetting the mare attached to the plow, Eugene abandoned his duties and ran toward his pale wife who clambered across the clods of dirt that would soon be their spring garden. "What is it? What's happened?" he demanded, grabbing the panicking woman by the arms.

"It's Calvin!" she sobbed. "Oh my poor, poor baby boy. He's almost drowned!"

"What? Where is he? Tell me what's happened, woman! Tell me!" Eugene shook his wife until her head rolled around like a rag doll's.

"He's–he's in the house with–with Mr. Adams," she said at last.

Eugene dashed toward the plank shack, his heart twisting in fear. If Calvin were to die. . . Eugene didn't even want to imagine the possibility. Calvin wasn't dead. Nadine said he was *almost* drowned. There must be hope for him. There must!

He burst into the three-room hovel to see McCall Adams gently placing the soaked boy on his bed.

Enraged, Eugene stomped toward McCall, grabbed his shirt in both hands, and looked into the face of a man at least six inches taller than he. "What have you done to him?" he screamed. "What did you do to my son?"

"I didn't do anything," McCall tore Eugene's hands from his shirt. "It was an accident. He fell into the river and hit his head."

"He was with that rotten Indian kid o' yours, wasn't he?"

McCall narrowed his eyes.

Eugene's stomach clenched in fury. His heart pounded in aversion. His mind whirled with hatred. He castigated himself for allowing the boys' talk about God the other day to distract him from beating Drew.

"I'm going for the doctor," McCall said, turning toward the door.

Collapsing beside his pale, drenched son, Eugene gripped the narrow bed's wooden frame. "I'm going to kill that Indian for this!" He turned to see McCall stepping from the earthy home's shadows into the light of day. "Do you hear me, McCall Adams! That Indian has done pushed my Calvin around for the last time. I shoulda stomped him already for beating up Calvin in town. Now that. . .that. . ." He inserted a number of expletives. ". . .has done tried to drown him. I tried to tell Calvin not to trust him, but—"

When McCall turned around, he looked like the devil himself. Eugene, momentarily silenced, stared at the man as he stalked back across the plank floors. Before Eugene could comprehend McCall's intent, McCall grabbed the sputtering man's shirt, lifted him, and slammed him against the wall. The blow reawakened an old back injury from Eugene's past—an injury caused by his father's brutal blows.

"I already told you, Eugene Wilcox," McCall snarled within an inch of his nose. "This was an *accident*. The truth is, Drew saved Calvin's life. And if you lay one hand on my son, I'll see that Constable Parker skins you alive! Now I'm going for Dr. Engle, and I'm taking one of your horses to get him!"

McCall released Eugene as quickly as he had grabbed him, and Eugene resisted the urge to jump him. McCall Adams was half again Eugene's size, and Eugene decided to leave him be for the present. He would get his revenge when he saw Drew dead.

Eugene once more collapsed at his son's side. Calvin's wet, blond hair was pitifully plastered to his forehead. In the dank room's shadows, he looked as if he were already caught in death's claws. Eugene's heart pounded hard, even beats behind his eyes. His labored breathing seemed to fuel his fury. He gritted his teeth, and amidst a collection of expletives, uttered an oath of death.

"Don't think I'll let a rotten Injun push you in the river and get away with it. I will make sure that Injun *dies* for this, Calvin."

&

"Miss Lowell! Miss Lowell!"

Kate turned from straightening her desk to see a shattered Drew, pale and panting, stumble through the doorway.

Her first thought was for McCall, and Kate's heart leapt in fear. In a flash, she remembered their final words. Tense, argumentative words, spawned by Kate herself. How could she have treated the man she loved with such contempt!

The man she loved. The man she loved. The man she loved.

Kate was in love with McCall! The realization hit her like a stallion's kick. She was in love with him. Was he, like Zachary, already snatched from her before her love could know full bloom?

The lunch of cold ham and potato salad crept up her throat, and Kate swallowed against a heave. She stumbled for Drew, damp and shivering, who had slumped inside the door.

"McCall. . . ," she choked out. "Is he. . ."

"No. It's n–not D–Dad." Drew rubbed his violently shaking hands over his ashen face. "It's–It's Calvin!" He clutched at Kate. "Oh, Miss Lowell! He almost drowned!"

Kate, collapsing with relief and horror, pulled the sobbing boy into her arms. "Drew. . .Drew. . .Drew. . .calm down and tell me what happened."

"I–I—oh, Miss Lowell, I know. . .know I w–wasn't supposed to meet Calvin. But–But we didn't m-meet much. Only. . .only about twice a month, and–and he j–just h–happened to be at the r–river today. . . ." Drew paused for a hiccough and attempted to catch his breath. "We were racing back. . .back and forth across the—that fallen log–g—*the log D–Dad told us to stay off of*!" he continued, his face contorted in agony.

"Drew. . .Drew. . .calm down," Kate soothed.

"I can't! I can't! Don't you see! He fell off the log and hit his head. I had to go in after him or he would have drowned. The whole thing is my fault. I should have minded Dad, but–but—"

"Drew! Listen to me!" Kate grabbed him by the shoulders and gently shook him. "Did you force Calvin onto that log?"

"N–No."

"Then you can't blame yourself!"

"Oh, Miss Lowell! I just feel so–so *horrible* about the *whole thing*!"

"Well you shouldn't, Drew," Kate soothed as she began

gently rocking him. "Sounds to me like you saved Calvin's life."

These words seemed to float around them and gently settle into Drew's mind to calm his nerves. As he clung to Kate, she continued rocking him in her arms and eventually began humming "Amazing Grace." At long last, Drew's weeping stopped, and Kate continued to simply hold him.

&

McCall arrived home long past the time Bob Mosely usually departed. He steered Eugene Wilcox's worn-out mare onto the horse farm and decided to return the animal in the morning. After alerting Dr. Engle to Calvin's situation, McCall had debated whether or not to follow the doctor and his nurse, Magnolia Alexander, to the Wilcox's or return home. He chose to return home. McCall wanted to make certain Drew was safe. The look in Eugene Wilcox's eyes left him far from comfortable.

If he had to leave his whole ranch for the sake of saving Drew, he would. Recently, Bob Mosely had hinted that he would buy the horse ranch should McCall ever decide to sell it. At first McCall had dismissed the whole idea. But lately, he began to reconsider. In recent correspondences, McCall's elder sister, Rebekah, wrote that she and her husband would love for McCall to move near them in Boston. If he and Drew were to move to the East Coast, McCall most likely could arrange for his son to attend a school whose teachers and students would better accept him. As Miss Lowell had clearly pointed out, Drew desperately needed friends. He was desperate enough to actually place himself in danger by associating with the son of a man who hated him.

Perhaps the solution lay in McCall's moving. Maybe a

close proximity with his only sibling would also begin to somehow heal the relationship with McCall's parents, still in Dallas. If his mother and father realized McCall and Rebekah were growing closer, perhaps that would instigate their rethinking former decisions. However, McCall also had Drew's future to consider. The boy did not deserve the danger that Eugene posed. If Eugene were alone in his notions, McCall would not be as concerned. However, other people in Dogwood felt as strongly as Eugene, even though they might never express their prejudice to McCall's face.

Wearily, McCall dismounted and gently cared for the old horse by settling her in a stall with a fresh bucket of oats and plenty of water. As he gently stroked her nose, he wondered how Eugene treated her. Probably in ways McCall didn't want to know.

Sighing, he shoved his hands in his riding britches and crunched across the hay-strewn floor. He savored the smells of horses and leather and straw, which were the essence of his life. A life he never thought he would be living. McCall had assumed in his younger years that he would spend his days in his father's bank, preparing to accept the reins from McCall Adams, Sr. But life had taken a different turn. In some ways, that turn had been tragic. In other ways, McCall enjoyed his existence with the horses. He had learned much about himself in the last fourteen years, including the fact that he would rather be outside with the horses any day than cooped up in an office. If he and Drew moved to the East Coast, McCall would undoubtedly glean his livelihood from another horse ranch, not the bank office where his brother-in-law presided as president.

If only Melody could have shared it all with him. A nostalgic chord echoed through his soul, and McCall's mind turned to another young lady who had been virtually dropped into his life. If only McCall could release his hold on Melody. He clenched his jaws and shook his head in defeat. The freedom to love again seemed an impossibility. McCall would most likely spend his life married to a ghost of his past.

He closed the barn door and walked across the dusty yard toward his log cabin. A lantern burned in the kitchen window, and McCall assumed Drew was either reading or in the process of eating everything in the pantry and everything from the spring house. That boy was beginning to devour enough for two grown men.

Thoughts of his son left him smiling fondly; then he sobered. Somehow he couldn't get Eugene's threat off his mind. He breathed a prayer and hoped Calvin recovered soon. He also debated how to handle the disciplinary aspect of Drew's blatant disobedience. Had he been "disciplined" enough by the realization that his friend almost drowned?

With a whippoorwill serenading the cool twilight, McCall stepped onto his porch and opened the cabin's door. Smells of freshly baked cookies and companionable laughter greeted him. McCall's mind whirled with the implications. He would recognize Kate Lowell's voice in a howling blizzard. She must have stayed with Drew for companionship. The thought left McCall thankful and agitated. He didn't think he had the strength to face Kate again. Not tonight. Not after Calvin's accident and all the worries that stirred.

McCall silently closed the door and made certain the metal bar latch was securely in its place. As he studied the sparsely furnished, shadowed room, he entertained the notion of tiptoeing into his bedroom, closing the door, and not coming out until Kate was gone. But that was impossible. She would need a ride back into Dogwood. Bob Mosely had undoubtedly already left, and McCall would assuredly be the person to escort her.

Stifling a groan, he lambasted his awkward predicament. Only one choice presented itself as appropriate. He would walk into the kitchen, face Miss Lowell, politely thank her for her companionship to Drew, and offer an immediate escort back to town. Setting his lips in a determined line, McCall removed his hat, hung it on the peg near the door, and resolutely walked toward the kitchen.

The sight that greeted him left an ache in the center of his soul. Miss Lowell and Drew hovered over the kitchen table examining a cookie sheet filled with fragrant, beige cookies. The kitchen, warm from the cooking stove, seemed to extend invisible arms and draw McCall into its heart. A heart that held his son and the woman who would make a perfect mother for Drew. Her dark hair, pulled loosely into its usually meticulous bun, was a bit disheveled and sprinkled with flour in spots. Her cheeks bore a faint flush, most likely from the heat of the stove. Her full lips turned upward in appreciation for the delicious smell. McCall knew the simple gingham dress she wore was a far cry from the fine gowns that must await her in El Paso. What made such a woman want to tutor his son?

"Drew, I believe we have been successful!" she said with triumph.

The boy broke off a piece of cookie and popped it into his mouth to gingerly chew it. He produced an instantaneous grimace and immediately removed the cookie from his mouth before Kate saw him.

"Isn't that too hot?" Kate asked.

"No. No, it–it was fine,," he stammered as he reached for the clay water pitcher near the basin. Drew grabbed one of the thick mugs hanging under the cabinet, filled it with water, and took a huge gulp. Apparently the taste of Miss Lowell's cookies did not match their looks.

McCall stifled a chuckle at his son's attempts to hide his aversion from the teacher he so desperately wanted to please. And their companionable conversation dimmed in comparison to the thoughts now bombarding McCall. He had been so busy fighting his own internal battles regarding Miss Lowell that he had given precious little thought to Drew's needs. McCall had thought he had done a good job raising the boy alone. A job Melody would be proud of. But he saw now, more than ever, that Drew needed feminine influence in his life, evidenced in this homey scene before him as well as the weekends when Drew anxiously awaited Miss Lowell's return on Monday mornings.

He was so engrossed in his thoughts that he didn't realize their conversation had stopped and both Drew and Kate were anxiously staring at him as if they awaited an answer.

"Excuse me," he said, stepping into the room. "Did you say something to me?"

"Yes," Kate replied.

"We were wondering about Calvin," Drew said, his eyes now downcast.

"Dr. Engle should be seeing him now. I believe he's going to live, but. . ."

"M–Mr. Wilcox, was he. . ." Drew trailed off as Kate placed a supportive arm around the boy.

"Wilcox is. . .disturbed." McCall chose his words carefully and exchanged a meaningful look with Kate.

Drew nervously drew a circle in a bit of flour beside the wooden mixing bowl. "Is it just because I'm part Indian that he hates me so badly?" he asked at last.

McCall desperately wanted to deny his son's words. He abhorred the thought that this child would go through life scorned for something over which he possessed no control. Although he would have never wished Drew into existence the way he came, this adopted boy had been a source of joy from the start. McCall saw traces of Melody in him every day. At first, he had loved Drew because he was a part of Melody. But then he grew to love Drew just because he was Drew.

"Do you know who my real father was?" Drew blurted, staring at McCall as if he were terrified of his own words.

Blinking in surprise, McCall glanced toward Miss Lowell who looked shocked herself. The question had come from nowhere and at a most inopportune moment. But looking back at Drew, McCall knew this was a question that continually haunted the boy. A question that very likely served as the source of Drew's recent distance from his father. A question that must be answered for his peace of mind.

twelve

Eugene Wilcox paced across the porch of his humble home. The doctor and his nurse had been with Calvin for the better part of half an hour. The boy awoke right before the doctor arrived and didn't much recall what had happened. Well, Eugene knew what had happened. That stinkin' Indian had tried to kill Calvin. Once the doctor left and he knew Calvin was fine, Eugene had a score to settle.

He wasn't the only man in Dogwood who hated Indians. He wasn't the only man who wished McCall Adams would never bring Drew to town. He wasn't the only man who would be ready to hang Drew for trying to kill Calvin. All Eugene needed to do was show up at the saloon, announce what had happened, and lead the way to the Adams' farm. Then, it would only be a matter of time before Drew hung from a rope.

The door rattled, then opened. Eugene stopped his pacing to turn and face the elderly doctor.

"Your son's going to be all right," Dr. Engle said as he scrutinized Eugene. "But he took a hard blow on the head. Magnolia is instructing your wife in caring for his head injury. I want him to stay in bed a couple of days. That means no chores or school."

"Fine. We'll see to it," Eugene said, anxious for the doctor to be on his way.

But the doctor wasn't finished. He pushed up his spectacles and continued to eye Eugene.

For some reason, making eye contact with the doctor left Eugene uneasy. So he looked across the west pasture toward the line of woods. The thick trees hid the setting sun from view, but the sky, ablaze with the hues of rich gold and rubies, proclaimed the sun's gradual descent. In the distance, a quail called out "Bob White" and another quail answered in return. Eugene wished he could whistle out a message to the Dogwood Township and have them just meet him at the Adams' farm.

"I hope you understand that what happened was an accident," Dr. Engle said firmly.

Squinting, Eugene leveled a steady gaze at the interfering doctor. "Why do think you know so much about it?"

"Because McCall Adams—"

"I know what McCall Adams says, and I don't believe him."

"Calvin even says he believes it was an accident. He says he and Drew are best friends and that Drew wouldn't—"

Eugene snorted. "What does Calvin know? He don't even remember what happened."

"I'm sure Drew does."

"Yeah! Like he *remembers* who started that fight in town last fall!" Eugene raised his hands in disgust. "Do you honestly think I'm gonna believe anything an Injun would say?"

"He's a good, honest kid. And yes, I think you should believe him!" Dr. Engle barked, his face dark with anger.

"And I think it's high time for you to go back home and leave us be." Eugene stabbed an index finger in the middle of Dr. Engle's chest.

"I'm going nowhere," the doctor said firmly. "My nurse and I are staying here to watch Calvin. He took a mighty hard blow to the head and—"

"*I'll* watch my son!" Eugene spit a well-aimed stream of tobacco near the doctor's boots.

The doctor narrowed his eyes, pressed his lips together, turned, opened the front door, and entered the shack.

Eugene debated whether to force the nosy doctor from his farm or to momentarily ignore him and ride into Dogwood. Forcing Dr. Engle to leave would certainly eat into the time that Eugene could use to round up the group of men who would help with the hanging. He decided to ignore the doctor for the time being.

That Indian had beaten up Calvin in front of the whole town. Now he had tried to murder Calvin. He should pay. The sooner, the better.

As Eugene strode toward the pasture to retrieve his horse, he cursed himself for not beating Drew the day he discovered him and Calvin near the river. Eugene had allowed all their talk about God to distract him from his purpose. Perhaps if he had used his whip as he had intended, Calvin would have never been injured today.

Only one solution remained to the problem. These parts didn't need the likes of Drew Adams. This time, Eugene wouldn't stop 'til Drew was hanging from the end of a rope.

❧

Kate watched the various expressions flit across McCall's face when Calvin posed the unexpected question about the circumstances of his birth. McCall first appeared surprised, then uneasy, and eventually resigned, as if he realized he could no longer put off the talk with Drew. Kate felt as if she wanted the kitchen floor to open and swallow her. She certainly did not need to be present when McCall told his son the truth.

"If you'll excuse me," she said discreetly as she stepped toward the doorway. Glancing over her shoulder, Kate wondered if either of them even heard her. They were both so engrossed in the moment that everything else seemed to have faded from their view.

Within minutes, Kate had walked onto the cabin's front porch, into the cool evening, and toward the summer kitchen. Her shoulders sagged with the weight of the day. Until today, Kate had not spoken to McCall in three months. Until today, Kate had not realized she was fully in love with McCall. Until today, Kate had been able to bar even Drew from the inner sanctuary of her heart.

She stepped into the dark summer kitchen and immediately lit the oil lamp sitting on her desk. Then she noticed Zachary's dried rose, still lying on her Bible, exactly where she had left it when Drew stumbled in to announce Calvin's accident. Kate picked up the rose and glanced toward the cold fireplace. Earlier today, she had almost burned the memento. Should she now?

Kate settled into the straight-backed chair, propped her elbows on the desk, and placed her face into opened hands. "Oh, Lord," she breathed. "Somehow, I feel as if I've come to a sort of crossroads here. I can no longer deny my love for McCall. Oh, dear God, I think I love him more than I even loved Zachary."

Kate's own words shocked her. She removed her hands from her face and stared at the rose until it blurred in the lamp's flickering shadows. How could it be that she loved McCall more than Zach?

Perhaps because you have revealed more of your real self to him.

The thought left her blinking in surprise. It was true.

With Zachary, Kate had been the person that her mother had taught her to be. Cool. Refined. Proper. With McCall Kate had done nothing but say the wrong thing at the wrong time and allow him the most inappropriate privileges, such as kissing her and suggesting that they should get married when he still loved Melody. Nonetheless, for once in her life she had spoken her mind.

Thoughts of McCall's proposal left Kate's stomach twisting in uncertainty. At the time of his hasty question, she had scorned the idea of marrying a man who harbored love for his deceased wife. Now, months later, with the full realization of her own love filling her heart, Kate considered the possibility.

Drew desperately needed so much more than a tutor. He needed a mother. He needed a strong woman who would step into his life and tell him she loved him unconditionally. At this crucial time, he needed the prayers of a godly mother. Even as she knew McCall was speaking to Drew, Kate wanted to be there for him, wanted to assure him that the circumstances of his birth in no way determined his worth.

And McCall—McCall needed someone with whom he could share his life. He needed someone to snuggle up to on cold winter evenings. Someone to experience his joy in the sight of a newborn colt. Someone to give him more children to love. And perhaps in time, Kate could somehow help him forget Melody.

With renewed purpose, she picked up the rose—Zachary's rose—and stood. Kate lifted the glass globe from the burning oil lamp on the desk. Holding the dried rose petals over the flame until the flower ignited and blazed on its own, she then tossed the blazing emblem from her past into the cold ashes of the fireplace.

In those moments, watching the fire devour her once-cherished rose, Kate felt as if God Himself entered her heart and, with the flames of His presence, purged the pain, the scars, and the heartache from her. Slowly, gently, with the utmost patience, the Force that created the universe had been performing a work of healing within Kate from the time she agreed to the tutoring position. In the place of all her fear, all her pain, all her haunting memories, He delivered Kate into a glorious freedom, allowing her to embrace the future.

As the warmth of the Lord's presence enveloped her, Kate's eyes brimmed to overflowing. Warm tears splashed to her cheeks and trickled to her chin.

"Oh, Lord," she breathed. "Give me the courage to embrace the future. And McCall, Lord. . .I pray the same for McCall."

As if her prayers conjured his presence, the door opened, and Kate turned from the fireplace to see McCall stepping from the night and into the dimly lit room. He silently observed her for several seconds, and Kate didn't avert her gaze. McCall Adams had seemed a man of shadows when Kate met him. A man of walls. A man of many secrets. The oil lamp's dancing light only made the shadows, the walls, the secrets, all the more prominent. He wearily rubbed a hand across his bearded face and glanced out one of the windows.

In the distance an owl called out "Who cooks for you? Who cooks for you?" Kate bit her tongue to stop herself from telling McCall that she would cook for him.

"Your cookies were terrible," McCall said, never taking his gaze from the window.

"What?" Kate hadn't exactly known what he would say to her, but she had never expected an evaluation of her cookies.

"The cookies. . ." He tossed a mischievous, sideways glance her way. ". . .they smelled delicious, but. . ." McCall shrugged. "Drew and I were wondering if maybe you substituted salt for sugar or something. Have you ever made cookies before, Miss Lowell?"

Suddenly the day's worth of tension seemed to spew forth from the internal bottle in which Kate had desperately tried to contain it. Moments before she had shed tears as a result of the presence of God. New tears stung her eyes. Tears of frustration, aggravation, and exhaustion. "If you must know, Mr. Adams, I have never made cookies before tonight. And I did it in an attempt to–to try to distract Drew. I thought I was f–following. . ." She sniffed. ". . .f–following the recipe Drew found in the kitchen drawer. I'm t–terribly sorry. . ." She walked to her desk, shut her Bible with a snap, and picked it up. "I'm terribly s–sorry that they didn't meet your–your—" Her voice cracked, and she grew angry with her own crying. Whirling to face him, she challenged, "Did you come out here for the sole purpose of delivering a report of my cookies? If so—"

"No. That wasn't even a part of the reason I came. I'm sorry that my teasing has so upset you. I never intended—"

"Then what exactly *did* you intend?" Kate would never admit to him, or even herself, that a large degree of her escalating ire stemmed less from his comments and more from the dire situation in which she found herself: She was madly in love with McCall Adams. Madly in love with a man who could never fully return her love.

Kate knew McCall well enough by now to understand what his narrowed eyes meant. *Good!* she thought to herself. *Serves him right if he's angry too.*

"I came out here to tell you that Drew and I are prepared to escort you back to the hotel now."

"Wonderful." Kate walked toward the peg where her reticule hung, retrieved it, and turned to face him. "I'm prepared to leave now, if you like." She desperately wished she weren't standing so close to him. She desperately wished she couldn't see the blatant admiration stirring the depths of his eyes. She desperately wished she could somehow reach into his heart and pluck the memories of Melody from his mind.

But only God could do that. Only if McCall would let Him.

Kate, snared by the moment, tried to gaze past McCall but couldn't. Instead, she greedily drank in his nearness. The magic the two of them shared since the moment they met now held her spellbound. As if he were as entranced as she was, McCall gently stroked her damp cheek with the backs of his fingers.

"Ah, Kate," he said softly. "I'm sorry. I didn't really want to tell you about those cookies. I wanted to tell you how lovely you looked, almost like an angel in the shadows."

She fought to swallow against her tightened throat. All vestiges of anger vanished in the tide of new, overwhelming emotions. Not only had McCall expressed his admiration, he had also called her by her given name, a name reserved for only the most intimate of acquaintances. As he stopped caressing her cheek, a cascade of tingles spread from her cheek, down her neck, and Kate fought to speak.

"I, too, am sorry. I'm–I'm s–sorry that I grew so agitated." To her own ears, she sounded as winded as if she had run a mile. "And–and I'm sorry about earlier today as well. I should have n–never been so snappy when you inquired of Drew's availability to work."

His silence only heightened the tense moment. Kate felt as though she might melt in the nearness of him. A part of her prayed that he would take her into his arms. The other part prayed that he wouldn't.

McCall, at long last, spoke. "I guess I should likewise apologize for some of the things I said this afternoon as well. . ." He cleared his throat nervously. ". . .when we spoke at the hotel."

His proposal sprang up between them and seemed to beg to be discussed. Kate, looking down at the reticule she clutched, chewed her bottom lip, and refused to mention the proposal.

"I should have never asked you to marry me," he said gently. "It was an insult to you and thoughtless on my part. I deeply regret many things about that day."

The pain in McCall's voice made Kate want to step into the circle of his arms, stroke his dark beard, and lay her head on his chest. She wanted to promise him she *would* marry him, and together they would work through the ghosts of his past. But she couldn't. Kate looked toward the fireplace where lay the ashes of Zachary's rose. McCall must burn his own roses before he could embrace her. Even if Kate were willing to marry him while he was still in love with Melody, she knew McCall would never expect her to share his heart with another woman, regardless of his hasty proposal.

"How did the talk go with Drew?" Kate asked, desperate

for any other topic of conversation. Much longer on the existing subject, and she was certain she would explode from grief.

"Better than I thought. Actually, I think this has been bothering the boy for quite some time. He hasn't seemed himself of late."

"Yes. I agree. I think it was time to tell him."

"I would be lying if I said he wasn't disturbed at all. But I think knowing the truth was better for him than being left in suspense."

"And you?" Kate dared to look once more into McCall's eyes. "How do you feel about. . .about everything?" Her question, though it sounded innocent enough, seemed as innocuous as a coral snake. Kate reeled in the torment from his eyes, glittering in the lamp's dancing light. That was one question he answered without a word. It was as though someone slammed the door on any hopes she held for McCall's complete, total love.

"Dad!" Drew's faint call echoed from the yard. "Dad!" This time the call was closer.

McCall turned to the door and opened it. "In here, Drew. I was just preparing to escort Miss Lowell back into town."

"Mrs. Wilcox is here to see you," Drew said.

"Mr. Adams, Mr. Adams," an urgent, feminine voice cried.

Alarmed, Kate turned toward the nearby window and looked out onto the yard, illuminated by the moon's faint glow. A slight woman ran from the log cabin toward the summer kitchen as if she were terrified.

"Yes, Mrs. Wilcox," McCall said. "Is everything okay? Is Calvin—"

"The doctor says that Calvin is going to be fine. But Eugene—oh, Mr. Adams, Dr. Engle told me to come as soon as we suspected. I'm dreadfully afraid that he has gone to town with plans to bring a group of men here for–for—" She turned terror-filled eyes to Drew as the faint echoes of galloping horses wafted across the winds of the night.

thirteen

The sounds of those horses chilled McCall's blood. He glimpsed the momentary flashes of torches through the trees that lined the lane. In terror, McCall wondered how many men Eugene had managed to enlist in his crusade. At once he pictured Drew hanging by his neck from a nearby tree, and McCall swallowed against a stomach that threatened to unload its contents. Yet he had precious little time for anything but action.

He stepped from the summer kitchen and grabbed Drew's arms. "I want you to go into the woods and do not come out until we come for you. Do you understand?"

"Wh–what? Wh–why?" Drew's wide-eyed expression twisted McCall's heart.

An approaching cacophony of whooping and jeering seemed to mock the boy's innocent question.

"Just do what I tell you!" McCall barked. "There's no time for reasons." How could he ever explain that Wilcox was using the accident with Calvin as an excuse to kill Drew just because he hated Indians?

A flash of understanding crossed Drew's features. Next, a hint of bewilderment. Finally, a deluge of horror. Without another word, Drew turned and lightly trotted toward the woods, his second home.

"Mr. Adams, I'm so sorry I didn't get here sooner," Mrs. Wilcox said, her voice trembling in fear. "But Dr. Engle and I were tendin' to Calvin, and I was a takin' care of the baby, and we didn't realize Eugene was gone for the longest. Then. . .then. . .I just had this most awful, sick feeling in my stomach, and the good doctor too, and. . ."

"Drew Adams. . .Drew Adams!" a drunken voice bellowed across the night. "We're comin' a callin'." A burst of raucous laughter punctuated the absurd claim.

McCall ignored Mrs. Wilcox's well-meaning chatter as his heart pounded with dread. If he had to, McCall would lay down his own life for Drew. He utterly hoped that, in his doing so, the boy could escape. Only when a soft, warm hand slipped into his did he remember Kate's presence.

"You need to go into the cabin," he demanded, looking down at her. "You and Mrs. Wilcox both."

"I'm going nowhere," Kate said firmly. Her face set in determined lines, she refused to relinquish her grip on his hand.

"Me neither," Mrs. Wilcox said, crossing her arms.

The dastardly group's torches now glowed in clear view. McCall touched the Colt Peacemaker that he had strapped on that morning before repairing the fences. Since the days were growing warmer, he never took a chance on snakes. Looked like the snakes slithering up the road on horses were the ones his Peacemaker would meet.

At last the trio of men on restless steeds came to a collective halt about fifty feet in front of McCall and the women. McCall, having expected more men, was relieved he must face only three. Nevertheless, the relief did not blot out his caution. As he suspected, a tipsy Wilcox, worn rope in hand, took the leadership position. The other two men carried torches, which lit their hate-filled faces and made them appear more demonic than human. Kate's hand trembled in McCall's, and he wished she and Nadine

Wilcox had gone into the cabin. Considering the trio's seeming lack of sobriety, McCall truly expected them to thoughtlessly shoot at anyone who crossed them.

Silently, he began to pray. To pray as he had never prayed before. To pray for a miracle.

"We come to hang that Injun!" one of the bearded men proclaimed.

"Yeah!" The wiry Eugene dismounted. "He done tried to kill my boy."

"It was an accident," McCall said evenly. His gut's quaking drastically contrasted his firm voice. "And you have no right—"

"You listen to me, Eugene!" Nadine called in a stern voice that strongly contrasted her mousy demeanor.

"Woman! What are you doing here?" Eugene peered toward his wife as if he only just saw her.

She closed the distance between them by half. "I'll tell ya what I'm a here for. I come to warn Mr. Adams 'bout what you were up to. It ain't right, Eugene!"

"Sounds like you're havin' trouble keepin' up with your own woman," one of the men sneered while the other produced a perverse laugh.

"You shut up!" Eugene snapped, glancing over his shoulder.

McCall began to wonder just how committed Eugene's cohorts were to their murderous task. He wondered if they had simply come along for the thrill of the whole wretched ordeal.

"I'm not gonna shut up," the petite, blond woman said. "You've shut me up for the last time, and I aim to stand my ground this time." She placed her hands on her hips in a stance that said she meant it. McCall had to admit he was astounded at her bravado. The few times he had seen them in town, Eugene obviously maintained a dictatorial upper hand in their marriage. "I ain't about to let you murder an innocent boy!"

Eugene, overwrought with fury, marched to within an inch of his wife as if he thought she would recoil. But Nadine, head held high, stood her ground.

"That boy ain't innocent!" Eugene snarled, waving the worn, gray rope for emphasis. "He beat Calvin up in town and now he's tried to kill him."

"Calvin started that fight, Eugene. He told me so! And I don't for one second believe Drew tried to kill our boy. He saved Calvin's life, that's what he done!"

"Sounds like your woman's got the best of you," one of the men scoffed.

As if the ridicule fueled Eugene's arrogance, he sluggishly raised his arm and delivered a backhanded blow across Nadine's face. With a cry of pain, she fell to the ground.

McCall's mind whirled with images of Melody, her face bruised from similar treatment, her cries of pain. Like Nadine, she had been a victim of masculine cruelty. Enraged, McCall stepped forward to defend the helpless woman whom Eugene mercilessly kicked twice to the leering cheers of the tipsy men.

But thoughts of Kate momentarily halted him. He whirled back to face her, picked her up by the waist, and plopped her back into the summer kitchen. "You stay in here. There's a pistol on the mantel."

"Yes. I have seen it."

"Do you know how to use it?"

"Yes. My father made certain of my abilities with a gun."

McCall hesitated but a second and desperately hoped he wasn't about to make a dread mistake. "Good. Lock the door. Get the pistol. And wait by the window. If you need to shoot, do it."

Her face pale, she mutely nodded, and McCall slammed the door. With the sound of the metal bar lock sliding into place, he ran toward Eugene Wilcox. Pulling his Peacemaker from its holster, McCall shot twice into the air. Not only did Eugene cower in fear, but his cronies also ducked in their saddles.

"Get up, Mrs. Wilcox." McCall stepped between her and Eugene and lowered his gun straight at Eugene's head. "Now you listen and you listen closely, Eugene Wilcox. I want you and your cronies off my property *now*."

"You're mighty brave for just one man," Eugene slurred.

"There's a woman in the summer kitchen with a pistol," McCall shouted loud enough for the men and Kate to hear him. "Kate!" he continued. "If anyone draws, you shoot them." *Oh dear God*, McCall prayed as the words left his mouth. *Please God, give Kate the guts to do what she needs to do.*

An unexpected shot, accompanied by the sound of shattering glass, exploded from the summer kitchen. McCall jumped, and Eugene covered his head and dropped to the ground.

"Get off my property!" McCall yelled. "Now! All of you!"

Although the men's horses pranced a bit, no one showed signs of retreat. McCall, praying like a mad man, decided on an alternative tactic. "Do you want to land in prison?" he reasoned. "What you're doing is against the law. It's wrong. And when you're through, Constable Parker will hunt you down and lock you away!"

Dead silence filled the yard. The only sounds were the chirping of crickets and that same, lone owl hooting at the night. Such peaceful sounds. Such a contrast to the deadly deeds on the verge of expression.

Eugene, still on the ground, looked behind him as if he expected support. Instead, a tired voice called, "Ah. . .let's go home."

"Yeah! What kinda man is afraid of a woman? He's probably lied to us from the start."

"That's right."

"I never did put much stock in what Eugene said no ways."

"Why'd we listen tonight?"

"Ain't no sense in hangin' a innocent boy."

The mumbling men turned their horses and, amidst more indiscernible discussion, began retracing their path.

"Hey, wait!" Eugene bellowed. Looking over his shoulder, he crawled toward his horse like a dog, and McCall resisted the urge to deliver a hard kick to the seat of his pants.

Another shot rang out from the kitchen. McCall derisively chuckled as Eugene flattened himself against the ground and the two horsemen urged their mounts into a gallop.

"Hold your fire, Kate!" he called, a note of approval ringing in his voice. "Eugene, get up and go home. *Now!*"

The half-drunk scoundrel stood, mounted his unsettled horse, and followed the retreating men.

From the ground, Mrs. Wilcox produced an agonized groan. McCall, still watching the group, helped the beaten woman to her feet. "Are you all right?" he asked.

"Yes. . .yes. . .I think," she rasped, leaning on his arm

for support. "This ain't the first time he's done beat me. I've lived through worse."

"You were exceptionally brave." McCall placed a supportive arm around Nadine and once more observed the trio of men, now heading up the tree-lined lane. The tension in his chest began to ease.

"McCall, is–is it safe for m–me to come out?" Kate softly requested.

A certain sense of intimacy rang in Kate's voice. To McCall's knowledge, this was the first time she had ever used his sir name. But then, he had naturally used her given name earlier without even so much as a thought. The two of them were certainly progressing in their relationship, despite resistance on both parts. What was to become of them? Would McCall ever be able to lay aside his past?

"Yes, it's safe," he answered, casting another glance toward the men whose torches now only occasionally glittered through the dense trees. "Come on out, Kate. Let's get Mrs. Wilcox in the house and make certain she's all right."

"I'll be fine," Nadine protested. Her right eye already appeared swollen, even in the shadows.

"You'll need to lie down for a bit," McCall said as Kate joined them. She, too, continued to watch the road in concern.

"I must g-get back to the baby and Calvin and Dr. Engle." Nadine made a feeble attempt to stumble toward the doctor's hooded carriage, parked near the barn.

"They'll be fine for the moment," Kate said, steering Nadine Wilcox toward the humble log cabin.

As she assented to Kate's urging, McCall could not resist the impulse to squeeze Kate's cold hand. "You were wonderful," he whispered.

She turned admiring eyes on him. Eyes that, in the moon's soft glow, seemed all the larger. Eyes that brimmed with love. At that moment, there was no question in McCall's mind that Kate Lowell loved him with her whole heart. With her *whole* heart. Several months ago in the hotel lobby, she had admitted the ties that bound her to Zachary. McCall now wondered if she had somehow released her hold on her former love.

A gentle spring breeze sprinted across the fresh foliage and promised yet another cool night, which contrasted with warm afternoons. The divergent spring temperatures seemed a metaphor for McCall's own feelings. At times, he warmed to the point of believing he could truly put Melody from his heart and embrace Kate. At other times, McCall remembered that cold chamber in his soul where those memories remained forever preserved in their chilling closet.

But tonight, with Kate's admiring gaze bathing him in love, McCall wondered if he were a fool for clinging to the past. Clearly, he needed to decide once and for all what he would do with his life: continue as a slave to the past or embrace a new future.

fourteen

Within an hour, Kate had settled Mrs. Wilcox into McCall's bed and encouraged her to rest. McCall, who had insisted that Nadine relax in his room, went in search of Drew. He promised to escort Nadine home upon his return. Kate supplied the scrawny, weary woman a cloth, soaked in cool spring water, to place on her swelling eye. Nadine uttered her thanks and shortly thereafter drifted into a shallow sleep.

Kate reached toward the oil lamp, sitting on the chest of drawers, and turned down the wick. The room seemed to shrink as the shadows closed in. Kate, her heart swelling in pity, watched poor Mrs. Wilcox as she flinched in her sleep. Only the Lord knew what the woman was dreaming. Undoubtedly, she had lived a harsh life with Eugene.

Stirred in sympathy, Kate breathed a prayer for Mrs. Wilcox. Much to her own surprise, she also found herself praying for Eugene. He desperately needed the Lord. For his own sake. For the sake of Nadine. And especially for the sake of his children. But he seemed so hardened, and Kate wondered if he would ever truly turn his life over to the Lord.

She turned to leave the room, which smelled of hair tonic and lye soap, but the dressing table in the corner caught her eye. Other than McCall's austere bed and chest of drawers, the feminine dressing table was the only other piece of furniture. Kate, noticing three photos on the dresser, picked up the lamp and slowly walked toward them as if a magnet were drawing her. Other than the three photos, only a yellowed, lace doily, a brush, hand mirror, and a bottle of perfume graced the dressing table. Kate leaned closer, extending the oil lamp toward the tarnished, silver picture frames. Just as she suspected, the photos were of Melody, and one included McCall as well. Perhaps their engagement photo. Kate set the oil lamp on the dresser and picked up the hairbrush by its whale-bone handle. Dismayed she examined the dark hair, which still clung to it.

Despair all but drowned her soul. Even from her grave, Melody clearly held McCall's love. Kate's eyes stung with fresh tears as she, at long last, comprehended just how difficult a battle McCall faced if he hoped to relinquish his past. Even though Kate had struggled to release Zachary, she had never been married to him. She had never known Melody's type of pain—a pain that had bound McCall and Melody even closer to each other. She had never raised his child.

Kate replaced the brush. With fear and trembling, she opened the tiny, square perfume bottle. Kate not only discerned the true depths of McCall's ties to Melody, but she also grasped anew the magnitude of his raising Melody's child—the child that many men would have rejected with their family and peers' approval. Truly McCall Adams was a man of unusually deep character. And love. Nothing with McCall probably ever ran shallow. Once he loved, he loved for life. Once he committed, he committed for life.

If only he could love, could commit to Kate.

She momentarily held her breath before delicately sniffing the perfume. When the light floral fragrance filled her nostrils, she sighed in relief. She had desperately hoped Melody's perfume of choice was not of roses. If McCall ever could completely love Kate, she didn't want it to be because she reminded him of Melody, not even in the choice of perfume.

A soft knock at the door left Kate jumping. Guiltily, she replaced the perfume's stopper, deposited it onto the dresser, and whirled to face the door.

"Kate?"

McCall's kind, concerned voice left her feeling all the more culpable.

"Yes. You may come in," Kate said, walking to the bed-side as nonchalantly as possible.

McCall opened the door and hesitantly stepped into the room.

"Were you able to find Drew?" Kate asked.

"Yes. He's in the kitchen now. He never had any supper. And even in the face of death, the boy is starving." McCall rolled his eyes and produced a slight smile.

Kate returned the smile but could not ignore the tired lines around McCall's eyes. "Do you think Eugene will be back?"

"I have prayed that he won't until I can't pray anymore. As soon as I escort Mrs. Wilcox home, I will escort you back to the hotel and alert Constable Parker to what Eugene tried to do. I am hoping the constable will invite him to a few days in jail."

"Me too," Kate said as she began to recognize a famil-iar fragrance, filling the room. The aroma of Melody's perfume filtered through the air.

Seconds later, an odd look covered McCall's face, and he glanced toward the dresser.

Biting her bottom lip, Kate sneaked a peek toward the perfume bottle to have her worst fears confirmed. When she had hastily replaced the bottle, it fell to its side, and the stopper toppled off. The yellowed doily upon which the square bottle sat now bore a damp circle, which filled the room with a sweet smell.

Kate stole a glance back to McCall who now looked at her. Obviously he understood that she had been meddlesome. This was evidenced, not only by the perfume bottle, but also by the strategic location of the oil lamp, still dimly burning on the dresser. She braced herself for the anger, certain to follow.

But McCall simply walked toward the dresser, righted the bottle, firmly replaced the stopper, and removed the soiled doily.

"I'm–I'm sorry," Kate stuttered.

McCall kept his back turned, and she wondered what on earth he must think of her. Certainly, the worst. "I'll–I'll wait in the summer kitchen until you are ready to escort me to the hotel," she rushed, forgetting about Mrs. Wilcox. Compulsively, Kate lifted her skirt and hurried toward the door.

"Kate," McCall whispered.

She stopped. Her legs shook. Her heart pounded.

"I understand."

Kate pressed her hand against her chest and fought to breathe evenly. Never did she expect such a response from McCall, especially after the way he reacted when he caught her looking at Melody's photo the day he kissed her.

"I guess. . .I have felt the same way," he continued.

Kate whirled to face him. "You mean about—"

"About Zachary."

She swallowed against her tightened throat. "I burned. . . burned his rose today," she rasped, wondering why she felt the need to tell McCall.

"Oh?"

"It was the–the last rose he gave me. I–I had kept it in my Bible."

"Are you saying it's time for me to burn some roses?"

"Not necessarily. I just thought. . ."

What had she thought? That perhaps McCall would like to know she had been able, at long last, to release her relationship with Zachary? Or perhaps by telling him of her release he would be motivated to find release himself? Even though Kate had not contemplated those exact words, she realized her motive had been exactly that. "Well. . .I just thought you might be able to. . ." She intertwined her fingers so tightly they ached.

A sad, strange mixture of sorrow, love, and regret poured from McCall's eyes. "You have no idea how much I wish. . .but I cannot seem to get past. . ."

Kate knew his words would haunt her the rest of her life. She knew this pathetic expression cloaking the fine face of character would be etched on her heart until she died. She knew, at last she *deeply* knew, that perhaps McCall could not, truly *could not*, release Melody. But before Kate accepted defeat, she chose to whisper one last request.

"I found a verse in the Bible today that I think might be some comfort to you."

"Oh?"

"Yes. In Luke." She struggled to remember the chapter and verse but could not recall the evasive numbers.

"The Spirit of the Lord is upon me, because he hath anointed me to preach the gospel to the poor," McCall calmly quoted. "He hath sent me to heal the broken-hearted, to preach deliverance to the captives, and recovering of sight to the blind, to set at liberty them that are bruised. Luke 4:18." He paused. "Is that the verse, Kate?"

Speechless, she stared at the man of her heart and experienced an overwhelming sense of panic. If McCall knew this verse and other verses and still could not release Melody, that could mean only one thing. Indeed, his heart would never be free of his deceased wife. "Yes, that's the verse," she said, feeling despair sink into her spirit.

Nadine's tired cough reminded Kate that they were not alone. Immediately, she wondered how much of their conversation Nadine had overheard. Her face heating, Kate looked toward the beaten soul in McCall's bed, but she continued in a light, troubled sleep.

"You should awaken her," McCall said. "Tell her I will take her home now. Dr. Engle and his nurse cannot remain at her house indefinitely, and I'm sure her baby must need her."

"What if Eugene is there?" Kate asked. "Do you think he will beat her again?"

The two shared a pensive gaze.

"I hope he *is* home," McCall growled. "I'll tell him I'll be back tomorrow, and if he has laid a hand on his wife, I'll make certain Constable Parker holds him in jail twice as long."

"But what about their crops?"

"I'll help with their crops or arrange for someone who will."

"You would do that for a man who threatened to kill your son?"

McCall produced a twisted smile. "If only I *were* so

holy. No. At this moment there are several things I would like to do for Eugene. None of them promotes long life." His scowl spoke of continued fury. "Nevertheless, I will do all I can for Mrs. Wilcox and the children. They are innocent in all this. Just as innocent as Drew." He brushed past Kate with a mumbled, "As soon as you can get Mrs. Wilcox awake, I'll be waiting with the horse and buggy."

≈

The next morning Kate arrived at the horse farm at the usual time. As usual she went into the summer kitchen and prepared for the day's schoolwork. As usual Drew stepped into the room and produced a cheerful greeting. But both of them understood there was nothing usual about this day. The shadows of the former evening draped themselves over every word, over every task, over every thought.

And Kate knew that Drew completely comprehended his predicament for the first time in his life. She desperately wanted to discuss everything with him, but she didn't know where to begin or even *how* to begin. Instead she cheerfully talked with him about *Romeo and Juliet* and hoped her smiles somehow comforted him.

By the end of the day Kate felt as if she had worked three days without sleep. Drew, unusually sober, likewise appeared exhausted. Even though McCall reported Eugene's escapade to Constable Parker the night before, all day Kate looked over her shoulder to see if Eugene was once more plotting senseless revenge. With every creak of the summer kitchen's floorboards, with every breeze, with every distant whinny, both Kate and Drew worriedly glanced out the window. By the day's end they had received no report from Constable Parker, and that could mean Eugene was still at large.

Wearily, Kate straightened up her desk and prepared for Mr. Mosely to return her to the hotel.

"Dad and I spoke last night about our moving to Boston where Aunt Rebekah lives." Drew listlessly stared at his math papers, propped his elbows on the desk, and placed his chin in his hands.

Kate stilled from her task. Her heart dropped. "Is this your father's sister?"

Drew nodded. "I've never met her, but Dad says she looks just like him, without the beard." He grimaced.

Under normal circumstances, Kate would have smiled, but she presently felt far from a grin. The reasons behind the father-son discussion were obvious. In the East McCall most likely would find a school in which he could safely enroll Drew. This would undoubtedly be advantageous for Drew. But once they moved they would no longer require Kate's services.

"When would you be moving?" Kate asked.

"As soon as Dad sells the ranch. He said Mr. Mosely might be interested in buying it."

A surge of anger, frustration, and bitterness swept over Kate. *McCall Adams*, she wanted to yell. *Why are you running? Why not stay and fight?* Kate glanced out the window to see Bob and McCall casually chatting by a corral that held a mare and newborn colt. From what Kate understood, this colt had come into the world with great difficulty. Both mother and colt received nothing but McCall's most tender treatment. He obviously loved this ranch. He loved the horses. From what Kate could gather, he had built a solid reputation for the quality horses he produced.

Why leave what he had worked so hard to achieve?

As McCall and Mr. Mosely continued their chat, Kate wondered if they might even now be discussing the sale of the horse ranch. New waves of fury splashed upon her. How could McCall do this? Or better yet, how could he do this to *her*?

Even after their disheartening conversation last night, Kate found it nearly impossible to sleep. Instead, she desperately prayed that God would perform a miracle in McCall's heart. Now, as she watched McCall and Bob Mosely's earnest interaction, a haunting realization struck her. God was more than willing to perform a miracle within McCall. But McCall had to *choose* to let Him. As long as he clung to his past, God could not do the work He desperately wanted to do. Just as Kate had to be compliant in relinquishing the pain caused by Zachary's death and embrace the healing that God generously extended, so McCall must likewise release the old heartache and embrace a new life. But McCall was not inclined to do that, demonstrated by his clear knowledge of the very scripture that spoke of healing. Obviously, the man knew the God-inspired words but had never applied them to his heart.

As Mr. Mosely ambled toward his horse and wagon, Kate placed hands on hips and stomped from the summer kitchen.

"Miss Lowell?" Drew's faint, confused call barely registered.

McCall, still gently stroking the mare's nose, didn't notice Kate's approach.

"Excuse me, Mr. Adams," she said firmly.

Perplexed, he studied her face. "Yes, Miss Lowell, is there something wrong? Drew. . .is he—"

"Drew is perfectly fine." She crossed her arms and narrowed her eyes. "But he tells me that you are thinking of selling the horse ranch to Mr. Mosely and moving out east. Is it true?" Kate scrutinized his expression to properly gauge his response.

"Yes, it's true," he said simply, turning his attention back to the mare who nudged his hand for a treat. McCall, his back to her, placed his boot on the plank fence's bottom rail as if to dismiss Kate completely.

In the face of McCall's obvious unwillingness to discuss the matter, Kate's bravado significantly abated. She scanned the rolling pastures, the lush trees, the dogwoods dotting the countryside, the numerous horses, all of which belonged to McCall. How could he sell such a beautiful ranch? The sweet smells of fresh clover and a clean spring breeze seemed to taunt Kate's very question.

At long last, she spoke again. "I never thought you'd run," she said simply, a note of disillusionment in her voice.

He spun to face her, a spark of ire in his dark brown eyes. "So what would you rather I do? Stay and see Drew possibly lose his life? Or see Drew facing a hopeless future with no friends and eventually no prospects of matrimony?"

"Surely you can't believe everyone in Dogwood holds Mr. Wilcox's opinion."

McCall quirked one brow. "I have lived here thirteen years. And yes, I can believe that the majority of the citizens of Dogwood are not fond of the idea that I am the father of a *half-breed*," he said with mock disgust. "I can guarantee that if a child who was totally white had dragged Calvin out of the river that Wilcox and half the countryside would have made him a hero. Instead, Drew has been turned into a murderer."

"Dr. Engle and Mr. Mosely *certainly* don't think that."

"They are exceptions to the rule, Kate. And while I know others exist who agree with them, they are by far the minority."

"So you're just going to run? Is that it?" she challenged. "You're just going to tuck your tail and—"

His face darkened. "I'm trying to make the best decision for my son! *You're* the one who told me he needs friends!" he said, waving his hand in agitation. "Now look what's happened since he made a friend!"

"I think Eugene Wilcox is an extreme case."

"Oh yes, Miss Lowell, you have been in Dogwood the grand total of six months and you have the whole citizenry figured out."

"No, I cannot boast of that, but—"

"While Eugene Wilcox might very well be one of the few who would blatantly try to harm Drew, there is a countryside full of those who breathe a sigh of relief because Drew has not tried to befriend *their* children." McCall pointed his finger directly at her nose. "Now you listen to me and listen closely," he said evenly. "Yes, I could do what you're saying and stay and fight, but what would it cost Drew? If I were the only one involved, I might do exactly that. But I'm not the only one involved. There's one other person to consider. And Drew's best interest must be the priority. I have weighed it. I have prayed about it. I have made my decision. Bob is going to the bank tomorrow to inquire about a loan. By the time Drew finishes his studies with you in a few weeks, he and I will move to Boston near my sister and hopefully begin a new chapter in our lives."

"So that's it?" Kate asked, tears stinging her eyes.

"That's it."

"Well, I must tell you then, Mr. McCall Adams, that you are dreadfully wrong on one count. Dreadfully, *dreadfully* wrong." A tear splashed to her cheek, and she angrily dashed it away. "There is more than one person to consider in this d–decision!" Kate's voice broke as her heart itself was breaking.

The dark shadows chasing through McCall's eyes attested to the fact that he accurately grasped Kate's meaning. However, he made no attempt to respond.

She stamped her foot in fury. "Do you know why you can't let go of Melody?" she demanded, so incensed she cared precious little that she was treading in deep, troubled waters.

"That is none of your—"

"It's every bit my business," she declared, her voice rising. "You haven't let go of her because you don't *want* to. You've set up a shrine to her in your heart and you'd rather live in the past than—"

"Stop it! Stop it! Stop it!" he yelled.

Kate felt as if every ear on the ranch must have heard McCall's outburst. She cast a furtive glance toward the yard to see both Bob and Drew, who had been hitching the horses to Bob's wagon, now staring toward them in astonishment. Kate, breathing the fumes of disillusionment, looked back at McCall whose stormy expression forbade her to push another inch. Silently, she wheeled away from him and stomped back to the summer kitchen.

fifteen

McCall turned his back on Kate and concentrated on the chestnut mare's gentle eyes, her twitching ears, her silky mane. He listened as Kate eventually boarded Bob's wagon. He listened to Bob's predictable "tch, tch." He listened as the wagon squeaked and quaked toward the lane that would lead them into Dogwood. Gritting his teeth, McCall deliberately dismissed Kate's heated words from his mind. Exhausted from the tension of the last twenty-four hours, he propped his arm on the fence's top rung and rested his forehead on his arm. All he wanted was a warm bath, a good meal, and an early, soft bed. At the moment, McCall had no desire to dissect his feelings.

He would take his son and move to the East Coast. He had survived fourteen years without a woman in his life. Drew would be fine once he developed some friendships. And Kate. . .Kate would find another love.

But what if God intended for you to be her love?

The tormenting thought twisted McCall's heart. If the truth were known, he *did* love Kate. He *did* think about her every morning when he awoke. He *did* pine for glimpses of her during the day. But every day McCall also encountered another woman who still lived in his heart. Kate said Melody was still there because McCall didn't really *want* to relinquish her.

Release the past.

That gentle whisper in his spirit disturbed him once

more. Could Kate have been simply reinforcing what God had been nudging McCall to do for quite some time? She was right. McCall did know all the appropriate Bible verses. But somehow, he couldn't seem to make them completely work for him—not the way they were supposed to. Perhaps it was because McCall was so busy gripping the memories and holding onto the pain that he couldn't accept the healing God was freely offering.

These thoughts took McCall exactly to the point he didn't want to be. He was simply too exhausted to examine his feelings. A bath. He needed a bath. . .and a meal. . .and the bed. He looked toward the western horizon to see the sun still a few hours from setting. However, McCall's body and mind didn't care about the sun's activity at the moment. He had been awake most of the night, alert, listening for any signs of Eugene's return. McCall needed some sleep.

"Dad?"

He turned to see Drew only inches away, his questioning expression asking for an answer concerning McCall's explosive reaction to Kate.

"Hey, Drew." McCall fondly placed a hand on his son's broadening shoulder and urged him to his side. The boy was undoubtedly on the verge of manhood, and McCall certainly was proud of him.

Drew mimicked his father's stance and placed a booted foot on the fence's lower rung. "We haven't–haven't had much time to talk since last night. I. . .hmm. . .but I just want you to know that I. . ." He swallowed hard as his eyes reddened. ". . .I love you."

"I love you, too, son." McCall blinked his stinging eyes and gazed across the pasture, bathed in late afternoon sunshine.

"After last night—after–after we talked. . ." Drew cleared his throat. "I never realized until last night. . ."

"I know," McCall said simply, at a loss for more words. McCall and his father had shared much less of a relationship than he now enjoyed with Drew. Nevertheless, there were often moments when McCall simply did not know how to communicate all he was feeling.

"And–and I want you to know that–that. . ." Drew stuttered to a silent impasse.

"I understand." McCall once more squeezed the boy's shoulder and the two stood in companionable silence. His silence declared a multitude of deep, masculine feelings. A dove's distant cooing seemed an echo of the years of love that had passed between McCall and the adopted son for whom he would give his own life.

"Will it be okay for me to attend school in the East?" Drew asked.

"Yes. I was planning that for you. Do you like the idea?"

"Yes," he said eagerly. "But what about Miss Lowell?"

McCall sensed that Drew was sizing up his reaction and he refused to look at the boy. Instead he fixed his features into a bland mask and focused on a red bird, perched on the corral's opposite fence. "Miss Lowell will go back to her home in El Paso, of course," McCall said evenly. However, McCall's heart seemed to wither at the sound of his own words, despite his resolve that her leaving them must be for the best.

"Don't you want to marry her?" Drew asked.

Pressing his lips together, McCall bit back a reflexive, defensive retort. Drew in no way deserved to be snapped at. But then, Kate didn't deserve McCall's yelling at her either. She had simply expressed her true feelings, and he had responded by demanding her cessation.

"I wouldn't mind if you did," Drew continued hopefully.

"Oh?" McCall turned to him, wondering once again if he should propose to Kate for Drew's sake.

"I think she's wonderful." The dreamy look in Drew's eyes left McCall suppressing a tired smile.

"Let's go in and scrounge up something to eat." McCall punched Drew in the arm and the boy returned a light punch to his father's midsection. They began their companionable walk toward the porch, but the sound of a horse galloping up the lane stopped both of them.

"Go on into the house," McCall ordered as he peered through the trees to see if perhaps the horseman were Eugene. Drew immediately obeyed his father, and McCall touched the Colt Peacemaker strapped to his leg. He had slept with the gun under his pillow and strapped it on first thing this morning.

Within minutes McCall clearly identified the horseman as Constable Parker. His worries alleviated, McCall slowly walked toward the wiry lawman. The constable wore his hard-as-nails reputation proudly, like a knight wore armor. However, McCall had long since seen beneath the constable's tough demeanor into his heart of gold.

He reined in his puffing palomino, and the high strung steed stopped within a few feet of McCall. The men exchanged obligatory pleasantries, then Parker said, "I come to tell you I've got Eugene in jail. I was also able to nab those other two characters with him. Seems they haven't been in these parts long and spend most their time at the saloon. I'm gonna keep 'em locked up awhile. Make 'em think about what they did really hard." He narrowed his keen eyes and rubbed his mutton-chop sideburns.

McCall felt as if a dark shadow was lifted. *Thank the Lord.* The last twenty-four hours had been nothing short of torture, constantly looking over his shoulder, never certain whether he should actually let Drew out of his sight.

"Thanks for letting me know. I've been nervous, to say the least. Did you mention to the Preacher Eakin about Eugene's wife and children needing assistance while he's in jail? I can help them a few days but after that. . ."

"You *did* decide to sell the ranch to Bob Mosely then?"

"Yes." McCall had made a vague reference about moving to the East the night before when he reported Eugene's threats to Parker.

"I really wish you'd reconsider. There's a number of folks that's gonna miss you. Might do you good to know that Eugene tried to round up a whole bunch a support for his scheme but couldn't seem to get anybody to agree. I think it's 'cause they respect you, McCall."

"But what about Drew? Do they respect him as well?"

Parker rubbed his sun-dried, wrinkled face and stared at the horn of his saddle. "I do. And I know the doctor does. He's a good kid."

"Yes. And I'm hoping that in Boston I can find a community and a school who will agree with you."

"Well, good luck," Parker said reluctantly as his mount began its usual prancing.

"Why don't you come in and join us for dinner? Might be a while before it's fixed, but we'd most certainly enjoy your company."

"I appreciate your hospitality." The constable gazed toward the north pasture. "But I'm headin' over to the Wilcox place to tell Nadine where her husband is."

"Tell her I'll try to be over tomorrow to help with the

planting," McCall said.

"That's mighty Christian of you." The constable produced a faint smile.

"Don't start admiring me." McCall touched his Peacemaker. "I was tempted to use this last night to settle this problem once and for all."

"I'm sure anyone would feel that way."

"I just hope Eugene can get a dose of what Drew tells me Calvin has."

"You talkin' religion?"

"Yeah."

"That'd do him more good than all the jail time in the world."

"I'll pray for him if you will."

Constable Parker smiled slyly. "You know my rule. You stay in my jail, you get a helpin' of the Good Book and a round of prayin' with every meal."

McCall smirked. "I like the way you manage your jail."

"Yep. I believe the Lord likes it too." Parker reached toward McCall, extending his hand for a shake. "Good luck to you."

"Thanks." McCall firmly gripped the thin, callused hand.

Parker tilted his straw hat, nudged his stallion with his spurs, and headed back up the lane.

McCall crossed his arms and savored the feeling of freedom. Freedom from worrying about what that vindictive Eugene might be going to pull next. Before Constable Parker's arrival, McCall had felt as if he were in bondage. He breathed deeply, relaxed, and savored the smells of horses and fresh spring foliage. As he turned to go into his home, he glimpsed the first pink blooms on the climbing rose bush that grew at the end of the cabin. McCall hadn't even planted the bush there. Before she died, Dr. Engle's wife had insisted the cabin needed a rose bush. McCall feigned a resigned compliance but secretly enjoyed the bush from the first day of its planting. Now, the bush served as a memorial to Mrs. Engle.

It also reminded him of Kate.

McCall stepped toward the bush and bent to inhale the roses' sweet aroma. The aroma filled his senses with the remembrance of Kate's perfume. He stroked the velvety petals and felt as if he were once again stroking Kate's soft cheeks. With the usual whippoorwills beginning their evening songs, McCall remembered Kate telling him she had burned her last rose from Zachary. He had asked her if she were implying he needed to burn some of his own roses.

At long last, McCall admitted that perhaps he did.

He retrieved the ever-present whittling knife from the front porch and cut one of the bush's blossoms. Holding it to his nose, McCall slowly walked toward the cabin's door and contemplated the last few months. The months since Kate. They had been troubling. They had been over-whelming. They had been. . .exhilarating.

McCall walked into the cabin to find Drew in the kitchen, the room darkening with the lengthening shadows. The boy was sitting at their small dining table, finishing off the leftover venison from lunch and the remains of the day's supply of milk.

"I'm assuming you saw our visitor was the constable?" McCall asked.

"Yes sir. What did he say?"

He briefly related the news about Eugene. "I think it would be good for us to go over and help Nadine around the place some time tomorrow."

"That would be great!" Drew said enthusiastically.

McCall grabbed a few pieces of the tough, salty venison and thoughtfully chewed it. He studied the rose, still in his hand and knew the time had come, whether he felt like it or not, to do some serious praying. McCall's back ached. His head ached. But most importantly, his heart ached.

"I'm going to be in my room awhile, Drew."

"I sure hope you and Miss Lowell can work. . ." Drew cleared his throat and stared into the empty milk mug. ". . .work out your differences. I really think she loves you."

McCall studied his son. "What makes you say that?"

"The way she looks at you," Drew said with an assured smile. "I see her looking at you all the time when you don't know it. Every time you cross the yard to the barn or come in from the horse pasture, she gets really still in front of the window. I usually tap her on the shoulder to get her attention. I'd say she watches you in about the same way I see you watching her in the morning when she arrives."

Speechless, McCall stared at his son. Convinced that Drew was a matchmaking schemer, he at last found his voice. "Have you by chance told Miss Lowell that I watch her arrival every morning?" McCall said, already knowing the answer.

"I'd bet if you asked her to marry you, she'd say 'yes.'" Drew barely paused for a breath. "Then she could go out East with us." His wide-eyed honesty left McCall reminiscent of the years he had watched the boy grow up.

"Thanks for letting me know your thoughts on the subject, son," he said with a fond smile. If only Drew understood there was much more involved than McCall simply asking for Miss Lowell's hand in marriage. Kate would marry him if he, like her, had burned his roses.

"After you have your bath tonight, draw me up a tub full too, would you?" McCall asked, turning for his room. "Until then, I need some time alone."

"Sure Dad," Drew said, a note of discouragement in his voice.

McCall walked the short distance into his bedroom, shut the door, and collapsed to his knees beside his bed.

Release the past. Release the past. Release the past.

In the last few months, those three words had become a chant in McCall's soul. He remembered Kate's words from only hours ago. *You haven't let go of her because you don't want to. You've set up a shrine to her in your heart and you'd rather live in the past than. . .* At that point, McCall had rudely cut her off. He rehearsed the scripture that he had quoted from memory. The words of Jesus Christ himself, *The Spirit of the Lord is upon me, because he hath anointed me to preach the gospel to the poor; he hath sent me to heal the brokenhearted, to preach deliverance to the captives, and recovering of sight to the blind, to set at liberty them that are bruised.*

To set at liberty them that are bruised. McCall was certainly one who had been bruised. One who had been brokenhearted. One who needed healing. The time had come for him to release his pain and embrace that healing. The time to remove the shrine to Melody. The time to burn his roses.

Drew needed a mother. Kate needed a husband. McCall needed—*desperately* needed—Kate. He wanted her lying beside him in the morning when he awoke. He wanted her smile to brighten his every day. He wanted her love to fill his heart, *all* his heart.

"Oh, Dear God," McCall prayed. "Please deliver me." The words felt as if they were pulled from his soul like an embedded, rusty chain that had held him captive. "Take my dreams of life with Melody, oh, Lord. Heal me. Free me from the wounds of the past. Teach me, dear God, to embrace your healing. Forgive me for thinking I had to hold onto my pain when I know You wanted to free me. Oh, Jesus, my deliverer, heal my broken heart."

McCall wasn't certain how long he stayed on his knees embracing the presence of Jesus Christ, allowing the Lord to enfold him. But, at long last, McCall felt as if he were truly communing with his Heavenly Father. He realized that, in the years following Melody's death, he had somehow allowed the pain of that situation to create a wall between him and everyone, including God. True, God had dealt with him and had empowered him to forgive those he found most difficult to forgive—including the man who raped Melody, and his own rejecting family. But McCall had stopped at the point of fully committing his whole heart to God.

When the long shadows turned to dusk and the last glimpses of gold stretched across the sky, McCall stood and lit his oil lamp. He turned to the dresser, Melody's dresser, and began to burn his roses. Piece by piece, he removed Melody's cherished mementos—the photos, the perfume, the brush and mirror—and laid them on his bed's patchwork quilt. He opened the dresser drawers and extracted the few pieces of her clothing to which he had clung, including the gown in which she died and a blue lacy shawl. He spread the shawl on the bed and filled it with the belongings he once had hoarded. With a shuddering breath, McCall secured the shawl into a tight knot and purposefully walked to Drew's room. The boy would one day be glad of these few possessions, a reminder of the woman who selflessly bore him.

sixteen

The next morning, Kate busily packed her trunk and arranged for transportation to the train station. She was scheduled to catch the westbound 8:10 for El Paso. Six months before, Kate had planned to take the same route back home. But this time, she would get on that train, no matter what. Once more she wore her meticulous blue traveling frock, her ivory brooch, and the plumed hat.

Before sitting down to pen her goodbye notes to Drew and McCall, Kate glanced at her reflection in the round mirror that hung over the dressing table. She was appalled, truly appalled, at the young woman who stared back at her. A woman with puffy, red eyes, marred by dark circles beneath them. A woman with pale cheeks. A woman who looked as if she had sobbed all night.

Yet that was exactly what Kate had done.

By the time the morning's weak light eased onto the horizon, Kate had made her tearful decision. She was going back home to El Paso. This time, she meant it. She would no longer submit herself to the humiliating fact that McCall Adams knew she loved him while he was unable, or perhaps even unwilling, to fully return her love.

She sat down at the small correspondence table and snatched a piece of paper from the drawer. After much deliberation, Kate decided to simply write a note to Drew. He would tell his father she was not returning. That would be sufficient communication for McCall. Up until she

165

started writing the brief note to Drew, Kate mistakenly assumed she was out of tears. But for every word she penned, a new tear seeped from the corners of her eyes.

She simply told Drew that she would not be back. That she did care very deeply for him. That she wished him the best on the East Coast. And that she would always remember him.

Within a matter of minutes, Kate's trunk was taken downstairs to await her in the hired carriage. She arranged for the letter to be delivered to Drew, and she rode the short distance to the train station. Although her heart felt as if it were being wrenched from her chest, Kate was certain she had no other choice in the matter. She had done everything she knew to do in relation to McCall, short of throwing herself at his feet and begging him to love her. That was the one thing Kate was not prepared to do. He had chosen to go to the East Coast without her. Therefore, Kate would behave in the way her mother had instructed. She would preserve her own dignity. She would quietly return home.

❧

"I am here to speak with Miss Kate Lowell," McCall said as he stepped up to the hotel receptionist's desk. He clutched the bouquet of pink roses he had clipped from the trellis beside the cabin that very morning.

"Good morning, Mr. Adams," the aging receptionist said. She eyed McCall with the same curiosity she had on the day she eavesdropped on his and Kate's conversation in the lobby. "I'm sorry, but you've missed Miss Lowell. She has checked out."

"Checked out!" McCall's shocked reply resonated off the lobby walls. A nauseating knot of nerves tightened in the pit of his stomach.

"Yes, I'm afraid so," the receptionist said as if she were immensely enjoying this drama. "And I believe she hired a carriage to take her to the train station."

"The train station?" McCall echoed in bewilderment. He thought he had planned the whole proposal to perfection. He had dressed in one of his banking suits and arrived in Bob Mosely's place to pick up Kate. He had intended to meet her at the base of the stairs, roses in hand. He had arranged to have a special table set up at Dotty's for an early morning tryst. Just the two of them. With hot coffee and cinnamon rolls, the very thing they had eaten that first day they met. McCall had even rehearsed the words he would say to Kate until he had them memorized to perfection.

Now she was gone!

"What time does her train leave? Do you know?" He pulled his pocket watch out of his formal vest to see that it was about 7:55.

"I believe she mentioned leaving on the 8:10." As if the train had been awaiting that exact moment to announce its arrival, a faint whistle sounded in the distance. "That should be it." The receptionist's wrinkled cheeks seemed to glow with the intrigue of the moment.

"Thanks." McCall rushed toward the beveled glass doors.

"Oh, sir! Mr. Adams! The young lady left a note, I believe for a Drew Adams. Isn't that your son?"

McCall wheeled around, raced across the polished wooden floors, grabbed the note, and whirled back toward the door. Within seconds, he jumped into his buggy and urged his trusty gelding forward. After but a few minutes, the train station came into view. McCall parked the buggy in front of the tidy, red building, tethered his horse, and rushed to the back where the passengers were ready to board the 8:10 as it swiftly approached.

Still clutching the bouquet of roses, he scanned the small crowd until he spotted Kate sitting on the bench outside the ticket window. Her head lowered. Her gloved hands clasped tightly in her lap. Her shoulders drooped.

McCall wanted to rush forward, wrap his arms around Kate, and pour his heart out to her. But with the westbound train chugging into the station, he hesitated. What if she rejected him?

Kate stood, her head still bent as if she were ready to collapse with a load of sorrow. McCall knew the sorrow was a direct result of his cold treatment the day before. Could she ever forgive him? Whispering a prayer for courage, he silently approached her.

≈

Her eyes stinging anew, Kate watched the hammering, squeaking train wheels as they slowly churned across the tracks. She felt as if those steel disks were smashing her heart, and Kate fought the urge to reverse her decision, race back to the hotel room, and continue tutoring Drew until he and McCall moved. Leaving now allowed Kate to salvage her pride. But was that worth the irrevocable separation from the man she loved and his charming son? Perhaps if she continued praying for McCall he would be able to put his past behind him and fully embrace a new love for Kate.

The idea of prayer marred Kate's thoughts with guilt. During the long, shadowed hours she had lain awake and sobbed, Kate never once sought God about whether she should go back home now or stay. As she reflected over those dismal hours, Kate admitted that her soul had wailed to God for comfort while purposefully avoiding the subject of whether she should go now or stay. For in past weeks, every time Kate asked God, He impressed upon her to stay. Still, McCall's recent rejection proved much too painful for her to remain in Dogwood, regardless of what that gentle, persistent voice within her said.

Amidst the hissing of steam, the train finally came to a complete stop and several of those waiting on the boardwalk began waving wildly at passengers who peered out the numerous windows. Kate knew that, many hours down the tracks, her mother, father, and sisters would await her. But Kate would be forced to feign her pleasure at arriving back in El Paso, for deep in her heart she wanted to stay. She wanted to embrace McCall. She wanted to arrive on the East Coast as his new bride.

Her stomach clenched. Her chest tightened. Her mind whirled with possibilities of staying. No one was forcing Kate to leave. Only her own pride.

Impulsively she turned to rush into the ticket office and reclaim her trunk. But she only took three steps and stopped. For standing only a few inches from her, McCall Adams offered a burgeoning bouquet of pink roses and an apologetic smile.

❧

Awkwardly McCall extended the roses. Kate stared at the flowers for what felt like an eternity. At last, she lifted her swollen eyes to McCall. Eyes that looked as though they had shed enough tears to fill an ocean. McCall knew nothing to say. He simply bathed her in the warmth of his loving gaze and hoped Kate could see that she now held his *whole* heart in her hands.

The fragrance of these first spring roses mixed with the soft scent of Kate's perfume and teased McCall's senses.

"I'm–I"m sorry about yesterday afternoon," he said at last. "I should have never yelled at you. You were right in what you said. Absolutely right."

Her lips trembling, her eyes filling with unshed tears, Kate covered her mouth with the tips of her shaking, gloved fingers and produced a mute nod.

"And–and I hope you understand that I–*I love you*," McCall whispered, his heart pounding.

Another silent nod. A wobbly smile.

"I've burned my roses, Kate," he said, his own throat thick. "And we can create fresh, new roses together. . ." McCall raised the bouquet for added emphasis. ". . .if. . .if you will marry me."

"Yes," she blurted, her smile turning to laughter. "Yes, yes, yes!"

McCall, oblivious to the curious crowd, bent and kissed her damp cheek, then pulled her into the circle of his arms. "Ah Kate," he whispered in her ear. "Promise me you won't ever leave again."

"I promise." She placed quivering hands on either side of his face and gently stroked his beard. "Till death do us part."

A Letter To Our Readers

Dear Reader:

In order that we might better contribute to your reading enjoyment, we would appreciate your taking a few minutes to respond to the following questions. We welcome your comments and read each form and letter we receive. When completed, please return to the following:

Rebecca Germany, Fiction Editor
Heartsong Presents
PO Box 719
Uhrichsville, Ohio 44683

1. Did you enjoy reading *Texas Rose?*
   ☐ Very much. I would like to see more books by this author!
   ☐ Moderately
   I would have enjoyed it more if _____

   _____

   _____

2. Are you a member of **Heartsong Presents**? Yes ☐ No ☐
   If no, where did you purchase this book?_____

   _____

3. How would you rate, on a scale from 1 (poor) to 5 (superior), the cover design?_____

4. On a scale from 1 (poor) to 10 (superior), please rate the following elements.

   _____ Heroine   _____ Plot

   _____ Hero   _____ Inspirational theme

   _____ Setting   _____ Secondary characters

5. These characters were special because_____

_____

_____

6. How has this book inspired your life?_____

_____

_____

7. What settings would you like to see covered in future **Heartsong Presents** books?_____

_____

_____

8. What are some inspirational themes you would like to see treated in future books?_____

_____

_____

9. Would you be interested in reading other **Heartsong Presents** titles?   Yes ❏   No ❏

10. Please check your age range:
    ❏ Under 18   ❏ 18-24   ❏ 25-34
    ❏ 35-45   ❏ 46-55   ❏ Over 55

11. How many hours per week do you read?_____

Name _____

Occupation _____

Address _____

City _____ State _____ Zip _____

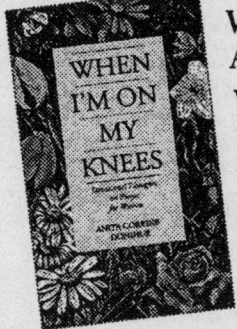

·······Presents·······

Great Inspirational Romance at a Great Price!

Heartsong Presents books are inspirational romances in contemporary and historical settings, designed to give you an enjoyable, spirit-lifting reading experience. You can choose wonderfully written titles from some of today's best authors like Peggy Darty, Sally Laity, Tracie Peterson, Colleen L. Reece, Lauraine Snelling, and many others.

When ordering quantities less than twelve, above titles are $2.95 each.
Not all titles may be available at time of order.

Hearts♥ng Presents
Love Stories Are Rated G!

That's for godly, gratifying, and of course, great! If you love a thrilling love story, but don't appreciate the sordidness of some popular paperback romances, **Heartsong Presents** is for you. In fact, **Heartsong Presents** is the *only inspirational romance book club*, the only one featuring love stories where Christian faith is the primary ingredient in a marriage relationship.

Sign up today to receive your first set of four, never before published Christian romances. Send no money now; you will receive a bill with the first shipment. You may cancel at any time without obligation, and if you aren't completely satisfied with any selection, you may return the books for an immediate refund!

Imagine. . .four new romances every four weeks—two historical, two contemporary—with men and women like you who long to meet the one God has chosen as the love of their lives. . .all for the low price of $9.97 postpaid.

To join, simply complete the coupon below and mail to the address provided. **Heartsong Presents** romances are rated G for another reason: They'll arrive *Godspeed!*